SPECTRUM SERIES
PHONICS

TABLE OF CONTENTS

SPECTRUM

Grand Rapids, Michigan

INSTRUCTIONAL CONSULTANT
Mary Lou Maples, Ed.D.
Chairman of Department of Education
Huntingdon College
Montgomery, Alabama

EDITORIAL AND PRODUCTION STAFF
Series Editor: Joyce R. Rhymer; *Project Editor:* Connie Johnson Long; *Production Editor:*
Carole R. Hill; *Senior Designer:* Patrick J. McCarthy; *Associate Designer:* Terry D. Anderson;
Project Artist: Gilda Braxton Edwards; *Artist:* Shirley Beltz; *Illustrator:* Susan Lexa

Frank Schaffer Publications®

Send all inquiries to: Frank Schaffer Publications • 3195 Wilson Drive NW • Grand Rapids, MI 49544

ISBN 1-56189-943-7   6 7 8 9 10 11 VHG 09 08 07 06 05

Organized for successful learning!

The SPECTRUM PHONICS SERIES builds the right skills for reading.

The program combines four important skill strands — phonics, structural analysis, vocabulary, and dictionary skills — so your students build the skills they need to become better readers.

Four types of lesson pages offer thorough, clearly focused, systematic skills practice. That means you can focus on just the skills that need work — for the whole class, a small group, or for individualized instruction.

The SPECTRUM PHONICS SERIES is easy for students to use independently.

Although phonics may be an important part of a reading program, sometimes there just isn't enough time to do it all. That's why PHONICS offers uncomplicated lessons your children can succeed with on their own.

Colorful borders capture interest, highlight essential information, and help organize lesson structure. And your children get off to a good start with concise explanations and clear directions . . . followed by sample answers that show them exactly what to do.

In addition, vocabulary has been carefully controlled so your children work with familiar words. Key pictures and key words are used consistently throughout the series to represent specific sounds. And a sound-symbol chart at the back of the text helps your students quickly recall sound-symbol relationships.

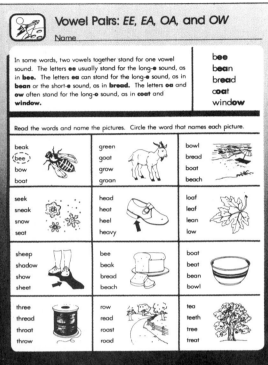

INSTRUCTION PAGE . . . The skill being covered is noted at the bottom of each student page for easy reference.

REINFORCEMENT PAGE . . .
Comprehension exercises that use context as well as phonics skills to help build the connection from decoding to comprehension.

Turn page for more information.

Easy to manage

REVIEW PAGES . . . Frequent reviews emphasize skills application.

ASSESSMENT PAGES . . . Assessment pages give you helpful feedback on how your students are doing.

ANSWER KEY . . . Gives you the help you need when you need it — including student pages with answers for quick, easy reference.

PROGRESS CHECK — Consonant Pairs

Name _____

Read each set of sentences and its list of words. Write the word from the list that makes sense in each sentence.

1. My family likes to *watch* _____ parades.
2. We always go early so that we can sit on a _____
3. The last parade we saw had _____ marching bands.
4. I clapped as I saw each one _____ by.
5. When I knew the tunes, I would _____ along.
6. I was surprised to see a float being pulled by an

march
laugh
thumb
watch
elephant
bench
sing
thirty
catch

REVIEW — Consonant Pairs

Name _____

Read each clue. Write **sh, ch, wh, ng,** or **gh** to complete the word that matches the clue.

1. a food made from milk — *ch* eese
2. something you blow into that makes a high noise — _____istle
3. a tool used for digging — _____ovel
4. two pieces of bread with meat between them — sandwi_____
5. a playground toy you can sit on — swi_____
6. hard to cut — tou_____
7. something you make when you jump into water — spla_____

shelf
both
wish
whisper
three
white
shake
change
think

Read each clue. Write **th, ph, thr,** or **tch** to complete the word that matches the clue.

1. something that can feel sore when you have a cold — *thr* oat
2. a number greater than two — _____ee
3. a picture taken with a camera — _____oto
4. a part of your hand — _____umb
5. a piece of cloth that covers a hole in a piece of clothing — pa_____
6. something that is used to make clothes — clo_____
7. something used to light a candle — ma_____

Review of words containing initial and final consonant digraphs

85

Prefixes

Teaching Suggestion 8, Page T–14   Extending Activity 29, Page T–22

Name Words to use: unlock, dislike, repaint, unload, discolor, repaid, overcrowd, mistreat, misspell, overflow, unwrap, distrust, preschool, unpack, rewrap, programs, misprint

Read each sentence and the word beside it. Add **un-, pre-,** or **over-** to the word to complete each sentence. Write the new word in the blank. The word you form must make sense in the sentence.

1. The *unfair* rules were changed. — fair
2. I **prepaid** the cost at the time I ordered. — paid
3. If you don't wake her, she will **oversleep** . — sleep
4. My dog **overeats** when there is too much food in the dish. — eats
5. Because I lost the game, I felt **unlucky** . — lucky
6. Scott talks about his **preschool** class. — school

Read each sentence and the word beside it. Add **dis-, re-,** or **mis-** to the word to complete each sentence. Write the new word in the blank. The word you form must make sense in the sentence.

1. If you *disagree* with me, let me know. — agree
2. Grandma will **retell** many of her stories. — tell
3. I often **misjudge** the time when I get busy. — judge
4. I will **reheat** the chicken soup for lunch. — heat
5. We saw the rabbit **disappear** from sight into the red hat. — appear
6. If you **misread** the sign, you will get lost. — read

Beginning Sounds

Name _____

Read the words and name the pictures. Circle the word that names each picture.

goat		van		came	
note		man		tame	
vote		can		game	
(coat)		tan		name	

fan		face		jaw	
can		case		saw	
pan		vase		raw	
van		lace		law	

Read the sentences. Complete the unfinished word in each sentence by writing the beginning consonant. The word you form must make sense in the sentence.

1. Please _J_oin us when we go camping next weekend.

2. You can ____ead the map to see where we are going.

3. We will begin our trip in the ____orning.

4. It will not take us long to set up the ____ents when we get to the park.

5. When we get to the lake, we will fly ____ites.

6. We may be able to go ____ike riding.

7. When it is dark, we will build a ____ire.

8. I will teach you how to sing a new ____ong.

9. Will you say "____es" and come with us?

Beginning Sounds

Name _____

Look at the pictures. Write the letter or letters that stand for the beginning sound of each picture name.

_f_ork

_____ail

_____ink

_____ipper

_____een

_____ose

Read each sentence and the word beside it. In each line, change the first letter of the word in dark print to form a new word that will make sense in the sentence. Write the word in the blank.

1. I went to a pet show at the school last _____ _night_ _____.   **might**

2. I have never seen so many cats and _____.   **hogs**

3. One boy had a _____ bird.   **walking**

4. A small boy brought a basket that held three _____.   **mittens**

5. Another girl had a tank filled with _____.   **wish**

6. I even saw a girl showing a pet _____.   **big**

7. The _____ pets were given prizes.   **west**

8. Picking the winners must have been a hard _____.   **rob**

Sound-symbol association of initial consonants; Words containing initial consonants in context

Ending Sounds

Name _____

Read the words and name the pictures. Circle the word that names each picture.

bib (circled) bid big bit		tab tag tan tap		can cap car cat	
bud bus bun bug		mat map mad man		hat had ham has	

Read the sentences. Complete the unfinished word in each sentence by writing the ending consonant. The word you form must make sense in the sentence.

1. Let me tell you what I di_d_ last week.

2. I too___ my first airplane ride over the city.

3. My ride was one afternoon after schoo___.

4. A friend of my da___ flew the small plane.

5. From the air I could see the tall buildings on my stree___.

6. Each car and bu___ that I saw looked like a little toy.

7. I could see the playground and the roo___ of our school.

8. Seeing the city from the air was a lot of fu___.

Ending Sounds

Name _____

Name the pictures. Write the letter that stands for the ending sound of each picture name.

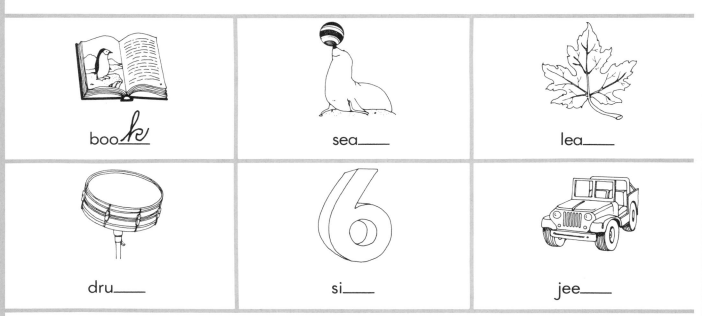

boo_*k*_   sea____   lea____

dru____   si____   jee____

Read each sentence and the word beside it. In each line, change the last letter of the word in dark print to form a new word that will make sense in the sentence. Write the word in the blank.

1. It is not easy to give my little _____*dog*_____ a bath.   **dot**

2. I fill a big round _____ with soap and warm water.   **tug**

3. When my dog hears the water running, she hides under

    my _____.   **beg**

4. _____ I try to get my dog into the water.   **Them**

5. The dog splashes me and gets me as _____ as she is.   **web**

6. Her _____ looks clean when I am done.   **fun**

7. Before I know it, my dog is in the _____ again!   **mug**

Sound-symbol association of final consonants; Words containing final consonants in context

Beginning and Ending Sounds

Name _____

Name the pictures. Write the letters that stand for the consonant sounds of each picture name.

_S_ eve _n_

____ a ____

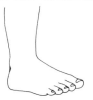

____ o o ____

____ o o ____

____ ige ____

____ e a ____

Read the sentences and the list of words. Write the word from the list that makes sense in each sentence.

1. The summer day was sunny and ___ _hot_ ___.

2. My _____ was to catch as many fish as I could.

3. I bought a _____ of bait at the corner store.

4. I took my bait and fishing _____ to the lake.

5. I _____ my fish into a pail of water.

6. The _____ was going down as I walked to my tent.

7. After a long day of fishing, it felt good to sleep on my

_____.

not

sun

lot

put

job

rod

cot

hot

get

Assessment of sound-symbol association of initial and final consonants; Words containing initial and final consonants in context

9

Read the words and name the pictures. Circle the word that names each picture.

tan (ten) tip top 	top tab tip tap 	tug tin tag tan 
ran rug run rag 	bed bag big bug 	clap clam clock click 
pen pat pin pan 	step stop ship shop 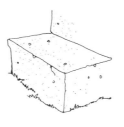	not nest net nut 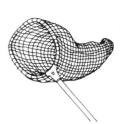
pig pen pin peg 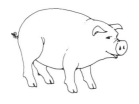	fans fist fish fast 	cap cub cab cup 

Symbol-sound association of short-vowel words

Short Vowels

Name _____

Name the pictures. Write the letter that stands for the vowel sound of each picture name.

bl_a_ck

l___mp

br___sh

ch___mney

l___ck

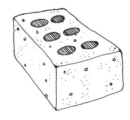

w___ll

d___ck

t___nt

br___ck

h___t

p___nny

f___x

Short Vowels

Name _____

Read the words and name the pictures. Circle the word that names each picture.

(tag) tip top tug	pen pit pot pan	hot hat hill hem
men map mop man	luck lick lock lack	lad leg lid log

Read the sentences. In the blanks below each sentence, write the words from the sentence that have a short-vowel sound. Do not write the words **a** or **the.**

1. These new red pants feel baggy.

    _____red_____   _____pants_____   _____baggy_____

2. My old hat is bright yellow.

    _____   _____   _____

3. My green socks have big stripes.

    _____   _____

4. I feel like a funny circus clown.

    _____   _____

Symbol-sound association of short-vowel words; Identifying short-vowel words in context

Short Vowels

Name _____

Read each set of sentences and its list of words. Write the word from the list that makes sense in each sentence.

1. Many of my school friends started a _____*club*_____.

2. We like to go hiking and _____ at nearby places.

3. Tomorrow we _____ to go on a hike through the woods.

4. You can meet _____ early in the morning.

5. You will get hungry, so remember to bring a _____.

6. If you need a backpack, I can _____ you one.

7. My father _____ take us to the park.

club
us
luck
camping
can
plan
stamp
lend
lunch

8. Jack's mom will _____ us home.

9. I hope we have a _____ day.

10. We'll talk about the hike the _____ time we meet.

11. Carlos _____ show us his pictures.

12. Sally might bring the _____ and leaves she finds.

13. Kim will _____ us about other parks.

14. We may want to talk about taking a camping _____.

15. When the morning is over, we can eat a _____.

jump
will
next
bring
rocks
snack
pick
sunny
tell
trip

Short Vowels

Name _____

Read the sentences. Complete the unfinished word in each sentence by writing the missing vowel. The word you form must make sense in the sentence.

1. I visited the farm animals l_a_st week.

2. I w___nt inside the big red barn with my friend Maria.

3. There I saw a large p___g sleeping in the corner of a pen.

4. Many young pigs ran around in another large p___n.

5. I could tell they liked running in the m___d.

6. It was fun to sp___nd time looking at the pigs.

7. Outside I saw a b___g horse.

8. My friend showed me how it could tr___t around the barn.

9. She also showed me how to br___sh the horse's coat.

10. The horse l___t me pet its nose.

11. Its nose felt warm and s___ft.

12. Now I w___sh I had a horse of my own.

13. I can't have one in my c___ty apartment.

14. So, I'll go b___ck to visit the farm again.

Assessment of short-vowel words in context

Long Vowels

Name _____

Read the words and look at the pictures. Circle the word that tells about each picture.

(bike) bake bite base 	cage code cone cane 	mile mole mule male 
rope rake robe ride 	like lane lake line 	nose nine note nice
cove cane cave cone 	rage robe rode rake 	cage cube cape cute 
dime dive date dune 	time tube tide tune 	hope hive home hike 

Long Vowels

Name _____

Read the words and look at the pictures. Circle the word that tells about each picture.

rise rope (rose) ripe 	skate slide snake slope 	home hide hive hose 
time tape take tide 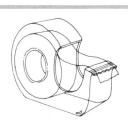	fine fake five face 	time tile tube tune 

Read the sentences. In the blanks below each sentence, write the words from the sentence that have a long-vowel sound. Do not write the words **a** or **the.**

1. I like visiting different places.

    _____*I*_____   _____*like*_____   _____*places*_____

2. Last June I visited another state with a friend.

    _____   _____   _____

3. We went swimming and rode bikes in a park.

    _____   _____   _____

4. I wrote a tune about our summer trip.

    _____   _____   _____

Symbol-sound association of long-vowel words; Identifying long-vowel words in context

Long Vowels

Look at the pictures. Write the letter or letters that stand for the vowel sound in each picture name.

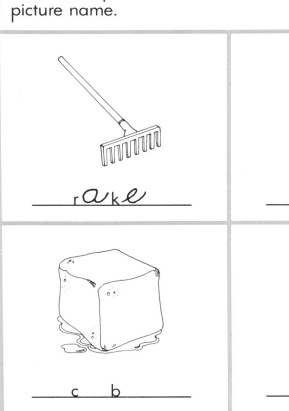 r _ake_ _	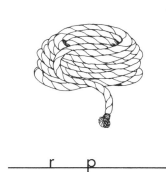 r __ p __	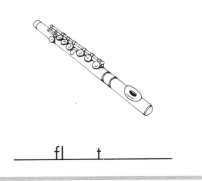 g __ m __
 c __ b __	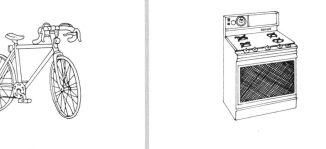 b __ k __	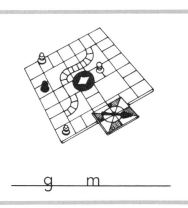 st __ v __
 n __ n __	 l __ c __	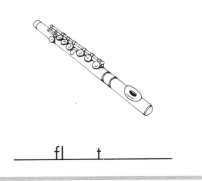 fl __ t __
 r __ c __	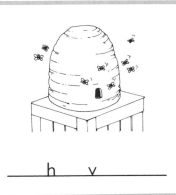 h __ v __	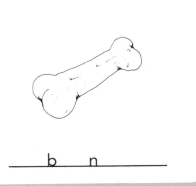 b __ n __

Long Vowels

Name _____

Read the sentences. Complete the unfinished word in each sentence by writing the missing vowel. The word you form must make sense in the sentence.

1.   It was l_a_te one night when I heard the noise.

2.   I had been sleeping, and the noise w___ke me.

3.   I didn't have a clock, so I'm not sure what t___me it was.

4.   The wh___te light of the moon lit my bedroom.

5.   I h___te to say that I was feeling afraid.

6.   Again I heard the s___me sound.

7.   I must have looked p___le as I sat up in bed.

8.   I felt myself starting to sh___ke.

9.   I remember telling myself to be br___ve.

10. I got out of bed and put on a warm r___be.

11. I called my cat's n___me.

12. A sound c___me from the toy box in a corner of my room.

13. Guess who had found a new place to h___de?

14. I felt myself begin to sm___le.

15. The cat looked c___te as she jumped out of the toy box when I opened it.

Long-vowel words in context

OLD and IND

Name _____

The letter **o** followed by **ld** usually stands for the long-**o** sound. The letter **i** followed by **nd** usually stands for the long-**i** sound.

c**old**
k**ind**

Read each sentence and words beside it. Write the word that makes sense in each sentence.

1. Did you get ___*cold*___ while you were waiting for the bus?

cone
cold
cot

2. When I got a new bike, I _____ my old one.

sold
soak
sock

3. Would you _____ going shopping with me?

mix
mine
mind

4. Little children like to _____ our puppy.

hold
home
hoe

5. Please keep your reading papers in this _____.

colder
folder
older

6. Were you able to _____ the button you lost?

find
fin
fine

7. What _____ of eggs shall I cook today?

kind
king
kite

8. Linc said to my teacher, "I am feeling _____."

find
fin
fine

9. Were you at home when Luis _____ you the news?

fold
told
cold

OLD and *IND*

Name _____

Read the sentences and the list of words. Write the word from the list that makes sense in each sentence.

1. It was ____*kind*____ of you to walk my dog.

2. The shop on the corner _____ balloons and kites.

3. The workers will _____ the meat while you wait.

4. I'm having trouble _____ my math paper.

5. Do you know where we can buy a candle _____ to set on our new table?

6. Visiting Denny was the _____ thing you could do for him.

7. After we do the wash, we must _____ the clothes.

8. His ride through the snowstorm showed that the prince was _____.

9. Would you _____ if I bring my brother and sister with me?

10. The park worker _____ us about the animals that live in the woods.

11. Seeing-eye dogs are used to lead _____ persons.

12. I keep all of my school papers in a large _____.

13. Which of the five bicycles is the _____?

fold

finding

told

blind

grind

holder

oldest

kind

bold

sold

mind

kindest

folder

Words containing *old* and *ind* in context

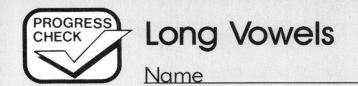

Long Vowels

Name _____

Read each set of sentences and its list of words. Write the word from the list that makes sense in each sentence.

1. Last spring I ___*wrote*___ a letter to my aunt.

2. I wanted to visit her _____ for a week.

3. She said it would be _____ for me to visit.

4. One night I flew there in a huge _____.

5. We were lucky that we didn't have one _____ day.

6. We spent a lot of time _____.

7. I wanted to _____ some rocks to take to school.

8. I found many _____ cones, too.

wrote
cold
nice
flute
outside
home
find
plane
told
pine

---

1. One day I helped my aunt by using a _____ in the garden.

2. For fun, I jumped into a _____ of straw.

3. Each evening, I fed the _____ calf.

4. Before the sun went down, I would _____ the pony.

5. After dinner, my uncle would play a _____ for us on his flute.

6. He showed me how he reads the _____ of each song.

pile
cute
grind
rake
notes
sold
tune
ride

Short and Long Vowels

Name the pictures. Write the letter or letters that stand for the vowel sound of each picture name.

f _i_ v e

_ l _ k _

_ s _ n _

_ b _ d _

_ r _ p _

_ f _ n _

_ r _ k _

_ g _ l d _

_ d _ m _

_ fl _ t _

_ p _ g _

_ t _ p _

Sound-symbol association of short- and long-vowel words

Short and Long Vowels

Name _____

Read the sentences. Complete the unfinished word in each sentence by writing the missing vowel or vowels. The word you form must make sense in the sentence.

1. The family garden is in b_a_ck of the house.

2. Every spring, I h__lp my mother plant the seeds.

3. First we use a shovel to d__g up the soil.

4. We use a r__k to make the soil smooth.

5. Then the seeds are planted in n__n straight rows.

6. The summer s__n helps the plants grow.

7. I pick every ripe green bean that I can f__nd.

8. We begin going to the market in J__n.

9. We t__k a lot of the food that grew in our garden.

10. The food is s__ld from the back of our new truck.

11. I put each person's food in a paper b__g.

12. Sometimes I s__t and watch the people.

13. The bright shining sun makes me h__t.

14. It makes me want to j__mp into a lake.

15. That's just what my d__d lets me do after we leave the market.

Short and Long Vowels

Name _____

Read each sentence and the words beside it. Write the word that makes sense in each sentence.

1.	We should _____*stop*_____ at Abby's costume shop.	stop step stone
2.	She will _____ us try on some clothes.	let led leg
3.	You might enjoy looking at the _____.	must masks most
4.	You'll also like trying on each hat you _____.	fin find fine
5.	I _____ to dress up as a big white bunny.	like lake line
6.	Dressing like a football player is _____, too.	fun fan fin
7.	My brother looks _____ in an elf costume.	cut cute cube
8.	If you want to fool people, wear a curly _____.	wag wig wide
9.	Wouldn't you look strange in long _____ hair?	pink pine pin
10.	If you want to look like a clown, wear a shiny red _____.	nice nose name

Short- and long-vowel words in context

Short and Long Vowels

Name _____

Read each set of sentences and its list of words. Write the word from the list that makes sense in each sentence.

1. When we ___*camp*___, I like to hike in the nearby woods.

2. I pick up each pine _____ I see.

3. I sometimes find a bird's _____ that is filled with eggs.

4. A small animal sometimes comes out of a _____ in the ground.

5. I carefully watch where I _____.

6. I want the animals to be _____.

7. Someday I will _____ a story about the things I have seen in the woods.

write

camp

step

ship

cone

mind

safe

nest

hole

---

1. My grandfather's house is near the bank of a _____.

2. I feed the _____ when I visit.

3. I like to watch them _____ around.

4. To get sun, they sit on a flat _____.

5. All the ducks march in a _____.

6. They look so _____.

7. I _____ I lived near a pond as Grandfather does.

wish

line

hold

pond

cute

ducks

swim

rock

stamp

Short and Long Vowels

Name _____

Read each sentence and the words beside it. Write the word that makes sense in each sentence.

1.	Randy will be _____*ten*_____ years old on his birthday.	ten tan ton
2.	We are beginning to _____ a surprise party.	plan plane plant
3.	Kristy will _____ our friends about the party.	tall talk tell
4.	Bobby and Sandy can _____ a cake.	back bake base
5.	Jeff will teach us a new _____ of game.	king kind kick
6.	Let's make a _____ sign that says, "Happy Birthday."	hug huge hum
7.	When it's time, Randy's grandmother will _____ him to the store.	sand send sent
8.	We will _____ behind the chairs in his house.	hid hide hive
9.	Jill will begin the birthday _____.	tune tube tub
10.	I _____ Randy will be surprised!	hope hop home

Assessment of short- and long-vowel words in context

Hard and Soft C and G

Name _____

The letters **c** or **g** followed by **e, i,** or **y** usually stand for their soft sounds, as in **cent** and **page.** The letters **c** or **g** followed by any other letters usually stand for their hard sounds, as in **cat** and **wagon.**

cent
(soft **c**)

pa**ge**
(soft **g**)

Read the words and name the pictures. Draw a line from each word to the picture it names.

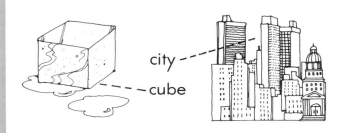

city

cube

game

stage

giraffe

garden

card

celery

pig

cage

calf

face

Hard and Soft C and G

Name _____

Read the lists of words. Notice the sound that **c** or **g** stands for in each word. Then write each word under the correct heading.

cent
(soft **c**)

pa**ge**
(soft **g**)

contest	goose	place	dragon	goat
price	cow	stage	cabin	calf
fence	guess	cab	gentle	judge
bridge	center	wig	edge	excited

Hard **c** as in **cat**

contest

_____

_____

_____

_____

Soft **c** as in **cent**

_____

_____

_____

_____

_____

Hard **g** as in **wagon**

_____

_____

_____

_____

Soft **g** as in **page**

_____

_____

_____

_____

Symbol-sound association of hard- and soft-c and hard- and soft-g words

Hard and Soft C and G

Name _____

Read the sentences. In the blanks below each sentence, write the words from the sentence that have soft **c** or **g.**

cent
(soft **c**)

pa**ge**
(soft **g**)

1. Gail moved to a city with a well-known bridge.

    _____*city*_____   _____*bridge*_____

2. The picture on that page shows a gentle giant.

    _____   _____   _____

3. The judge will hear the first case in this place.

    _____   _____

Read the sentences. In the blanks below each sentence, write the words from the sentence that have hard **c** or **g.**

1. Can you get the cat before it runs under the fence?

    _____*Can*_____   _____*get*_____   _____*cat*_____

2. We raced to catch the goat in the garden.

    _____   _____   _____

3. The cow was excited when it got outside the gate.

    _____   _____   _____

Hard and Soft C and G

Name _____

Read the sentences and the words beside them. Write the word that makes sense in each sentence.

1. Please sign this birthday ___*card*___.

2. We can send it to our friend in the _____.

city
cost
card

3. Read the words on the first _____ of this book.

4. They tell you how to play a running _____.

cage
page
game

5. Would you like a _____ of wheat bread?

6. Should I fill your _____ with milk?

cup
cent
slice

7. The park is near the _____ that crosses the stream.

8. Wing likes to look at the flower _____ there.

bridge
car
garden

9. When the play begins, I am standing on the _____.

10. She will sing a very _____ song.

wagon
gentle
stage

11. Did you like the animal shows in the _____?

12. I thought the monkeys were _____.

price
circus
cute

13. Do you like the taste of _____?

14. I can _____ some for you to try.

center
cook
rice

Review of hard- and soft-*c* and hard- and soft-*g* words in context

Hard and Soft C and G

Name _____

Read each sentence. Circle the word **hard** or **soft** to tell the kind of sound the **c** or **g** in dark print stands for. Remember: **Cent** and **page** have soft sounds. **Cat** and **wagon** have hard sounds.

1.	Where will the cooking **c**ontest be held?	(hard) soft
2.	There is a bicycle shop in the **c**enter of the town.	hard soft
3.	My make-believe story is about an unhappy fro**g**.	hard soft
4.	What kind of **g**ame should we play?	hard soft
5.	After he ran two miles his fa**c**e was red.	hard soft
6.	Will you help me choose a **c**andle?	hard soft
7.	Her father bought her a new silver bra**c**elet.	hard soft
8.	Lin wore a long black wi**g** at the costume party.	hard soft
9.	Do you know the pri**c**e of that football shirt?	hard soft
10.	The **g**iraffe has a long neck.	hard soft
11.	Stand away from the ed**g**e of the cliff.	hard soft

Two-Letter Blends

Name _____

In some words, one consonant follows another consonant. To say these words, blend the sounds of the two consonants together.

stop   **tw**in
play   **squ**irrel
green

Read the words and look at the pictures. Circle the word that tells about each picture.

(crib) trip grin drip	clock float block glove 	trap snap slap clap 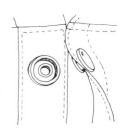
grown brown frown crown 	stone smoke spoke slope 	dry cry fry pry 
flow glow slow snow 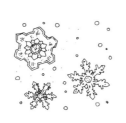	black clam flag glass 	spot slide stir squirrel 
twice twin twine twig 	flame plane slate plate 	draw tray gray crab 

   Symbol-sound association of words containing *tw*, *s*, *l*, and *r* blends

Two-Letter Blends

Name _____

Read each sentence and the words beside it. Write the word that makes sense in each sentence.

1. I like to roller _____*skate*_____ outdoors.

state
skate
slate

2. I _____ at my house and skate to the park.

smart
start
scarf

3. If I think I'm going to fall, I hold onto a _____.

free
tree
glee

4. I am careful not to trip on each _____ of the sidewalk.

crack
track
black

5. The smooth path in the park helps me to _____.

glide
twin
slid

6. My arms _____ as I skate along the path.

sting
swing
skip

7. The soft _____ feels good in my hair.

breeze
freeze
green

8. I sometimes _____ about flying through the air.

great
twenty
dream

9. I meet two people on the path and _____ between them.

sweater
squeeze
speech

10. After skating I am tired, but I feel _____!

great
cream
treat

Words containing *tw, s, l,* and *r* blends in context

33

Two-Letter Blends

Name _____

Read the sentences. Complete the unfinished word in each sentence by writing the missing blend. Choose from the following blends: **sw, cl, fl, br, fr, sq.** The word you form must make sense in the sentence.

1. Please help me ___*cl*___ean my dirty bedroom.

2. I will pick up the clothes from the _____oor.

3. Would you _____eep the floor with this broom?

4. My brother's toy _____uirrel is under the bed.

5. Here is the _____ush that I thought was lost.

6. Now I can walk _____om place to place without tripping over things!

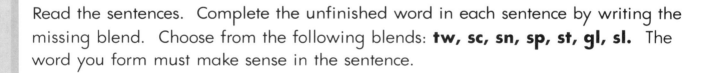

Read the sentences. Complete the unfinished word in each sentence by writing the missing blend. Choose from the following blends: **tw, sc, sn, sp, st, gl, sl.** The word you form must make sense in the sentence.

1. Grandfather will ___*sc*___old me if I get up.

2. He said I should try to _____eep.

3. I guess he heard me _____eezing this morning.

4. My _____in sister had a cold before I did.

5. She had to _____end two days in bed last weekend.

6. She told me that Grandfather can also tell a good _____ory any time of day.

7. I am _____ad that Grandfather is here.

Words containing *tw, s, l,* and *r* blends in context

Two-Letter Blends

Name _____

Read each clue. Complete the word beside it to form a word that matches the clue. Choose from the following blends: **tw, sl, sm, st, sw.** You may use a blend more than once.

1. something you need to mail a letter   _*st*_amp

2. the number before thirteen   _____elve

3. a toy used to ride on snow   _____ed

4. something you can do in a pool or lake   _____im

5. to mix food   _____ir

6. something you do when you are happy   _____ile

Read each clue. Complete the word beside it to form a word that matches the clue. Choose from the following blends: **bl, fl, br, gr, tr, cr, sq.**

1. the color of the sky   _*bl*_ue

2. a path   _____ail

3. a kind of fruit that grows on a vine   _____ape

4. something that hangs on a pole   _____ag

5. something that can be made into toast   _____ead

6. a shape that has four sides of the same length   _____uare

7. a loud noise   _____ash

Three-Letter Blends

Name _____

In some words, the letter **s** is followed by two other consonants. To say these words, blend the sound of **s** with the sounds of the consonants that follow.

spring
scream
split
strip

Read the words and look at the pictures. Circle the word that tells about each picture.

split (string) spring strip		strange sprang splash scratch		stream spread screw street	
split splinter strip strike		street scream stream spread		spray scratch strange sprang	
screech spread stream street		splash scratch straight sprang		spread scream stream street	
sprout strong scrap stroke		spray scrape straw splash		strange scrape splash sprang	

Symbol-sound association of words containing three-letter blends: *spr, scr, spl, str*

Three-Letter Blends

Name _____

Read each sentence and the words beside it. Write the word that makes sense in each sentence.

1. What a ___*strange*___ day I've had today!

scratch
strange
sprang

2. I _____ a seam in my yellow shirt.

strike
split
strip

3. I _____ butter on my hand instead of on the toast.

stream
spread
scream

4. My best friend _____ his leg when we were playing.

stranger
sprained
screamed

5. I forgot to get a _____ for my milk when I went through the lunch line.

strange
straw
straight

6. The _____ on my only backpack broke.

splash
strap
scratch

7. I ran into the _____ door.

stream
screen
spread

8. I got a _____ in my right hand.

splinter
strip
strike

9. A car _____ water on me.

scraped
splashed
scratched

10. I think I'll go _____ to bed when I get home!

spray
scratch
straight

Three-Letter Blends

Name _____

Read the sentences. Complete the unfinished word in each sentence by writing the missing blend. Choose from the following blends: **spr, scr, spl, str.** You may use a blend more than once. The word you form must make sense in the sentence.

1. Would you like to fix _____*scr*_____ambled eggs for Grandmother?

2. Can Brenda swim _____aight across the deep end of the pool?

3. Try not to make a big _____ash when you dive.

4. I used the hose to _____ay water for the children.

5. Last spring I helped put a new _____een in my window.

6. How did Jan _____ain her arm?

7. We plan to plant some flowers next _____ing.

8. Before winter, we _____it wood to burn in our fireplace.

9. Before we begin painting the house, we must _____ape off the old paint.

10. Scott let out a loud _____eam when you frightened him.

11. Listen to that _____ange noise.

12. Is Allan _____ong enough to lift this box?

13. The first time Billy was up to bat, he got a _____ike.

14. How did you get that _____inter in your finger?

15. Are there any fish in that shallow _____eam?

Words containing three-letter blends in context: *spr, scr, spl, str*

Three-Letter Blends

Name _____

Read each clue. Complete the word beside it to form a word that matches the clue. Choose from the following blends: **spr, scr, spl, str.** You may use a blend more than once.

1. to hurt an arm or leg by twisting it   _spr_ ain

2. not curved   _____ aight

3. something cats do with their claws   _____ atch

4. a wide brook   _____ eam

5. to hurt the skin on a knee   _____ ape

6. to wash with a brush   _____ ub

7. what water does when you jump into a pool   _____ ashes

8. something found in a barn   _____ aw

9. a time of year when flowers bloom outdoors   _____ ing

10. a tiny piece of wood   _____ inter

11. another name for a road   _____ eet

12. to yell in a high voice   _____ eam

13. to put butter on bread   _____ ead

14. to break something apart   _____ it

15. to scatter tiny drops of water   _____ ay

Ending Blends

Name _____

At the end of some words two consonants appear together. To say these words, blend the sounds of the two consonants together.

la**st**   sta**mp**
ha**nd**   gi**ft**

Read the words and name the pictures.   Circle the word that names each picture.

gasp (gift) golf gust	cast camp cent cost	soft sand sink sent

mast mist mask milk	pink plant pump pant	bump belt built best

 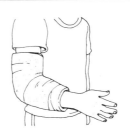 

rent raft ramp rest	bank bent bend band	lamp left lump lift

stamp stand stump stunt	shelf shirt shift skunk	skunk skirt shift shirt

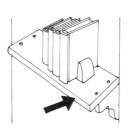  

Symbol-sound association of words containing final blends

Ending Blends

Name _____

Read each sentence and the words beside it. Write the word that makes sense in each sentence.

1. You need to put on old pants and a _____*shirt*_____.

   shift
   shirt
   shelf

2. I want you to go with me to see what's _____ in the old barn.

   lift
   left
   lamp

3. You can _____ me open the heavy sliding door.

   honk
   help
   hand

4. I'll see if I can find a _____ to give us some light.

   land
   lamp
   last

5. Look at the rusty tools on this _____.

   short
   shelf
   shift

6. Do you think Grandfather used this tool to _____ seeds?

   plant
   part
   paint

7. She wants to know what kind of bird _____ that nest.

   belt
   built
   bold

8. We will have to _____ our teacher.

   ask
   ant
   and

9. I can _____ him a letter tonight.

   send
   sent
   self

10. Let's go to the old _____ on our next visit.

   fast
   fort
   first

Words containing final blends in context

41

Ending Blends

Name _____

Complete the unfinished word in each sentence by writing the missing blends. Choose from the following blends: **lf, lt, st, mp, nk, rt, ft, nd, nt, sk.** You may use a blend more than once. The word you form must make sense in the sentence.

1. My friends met our family at the city airpo_*rt*_.

2. A strong wi_____ was blowing.

3. We ran to put the bags into the tru_____ of the car.

4. We stayed at my friend's home because we fe_____ it was too cold to camp.

5. First I put a funny ma_____ on my face.

6. Next I'll put on a wig made of so_____ yellow yarn.

7. I will wear a bright red shi_____ and baggy blue pants.

8. Then I'll be ready to go to work in the circus te_____.

9. Most of the books that tell how the old fo_____ was built have been sold.

10. There aren't many left on the she_____.

11. People must like the pictures drawn by the book's arti_____.

12. They sit at the de_____ in the bookstore and look at the books.

13. Please put a sta_____ on this letter.

14. I will se_____ it to Mom after we go swimming.

15. She will want to know about the ra_____ ride we took on the river.

Words containing final blends in context

Ending Blends

Name _____

Read each clue. Complete the word beside it to form a word that matches the clue.
Choose from the following blends: **st, sk, nd, nk, nt, mp, lf, lt, rt, ft.** You may
use a blend more than once.

1. a small lake   po*nd*

2. to spread color with a brush   pai_____

3. a tiny, make-believe person   e_____

4. what is left of a tree after it has been cut down   stu_____

5. a place to save money   ba_____

6. the part of the body that pumps blood   hea_____

7. the plaster covering on a broken arm or leg   ca_____

8. a present   gi_____

9. the opposite of right   le_____

10. something found at a beach   sa_____

11. a place for airplanes   airpo_____

12. a penny   ce_____

13. a group of people who play songs while marching   ba_____

14. a table used for writing or studying   de_____

15. a young male horse   co_____

Blends

Name _____

Read each set of sentences and its list of words. Write the word from the list that makes sense in each sentence.

1. Patty walks to the _____*pond*_____ in the park.

2. Her dog runs _____ her.

3. The dog likes to _____ water on itself.

4. Patty calls, and the dog runs _____ to her.

5. Patty _____ as her dog jumps up.

6. She throws a _____ into the air.

7. That dog likes to _____ "catch."

play

straight

squeals

stick

pond

splash

draw

past

plan

1. One day last week I was standing in _____ of the house.

2. I saw something _____ to move.

3. What was that _____ animal?

4. I moved slowly and tried to get _____ to it.

5. I was surprised to see a _____!

6. I've always been afraid of their _____.

7. "Oh, _____ don't let it spray me," I thought.

8. I was lucky that I didn't _____.

close

skunk

smell

free

front

scream

block

strange

start

please

Assessment of words containing initial and final blends in context

Silent Consonants: KN, WR, and SC

Name _____

In some words, two consonants together stand for one sound.
The letters **kn** usually stand for the sound of **n**, as in **knot**.
The letters **wr** usually stand for the sound of **r**, as in **write**.
The letters **sc** sometimes stand for the sound of **s**, as in **scissors**.

knot
write
scissors

Look at the pictures. Write the letters that stand for the beginning sound of each picture name.

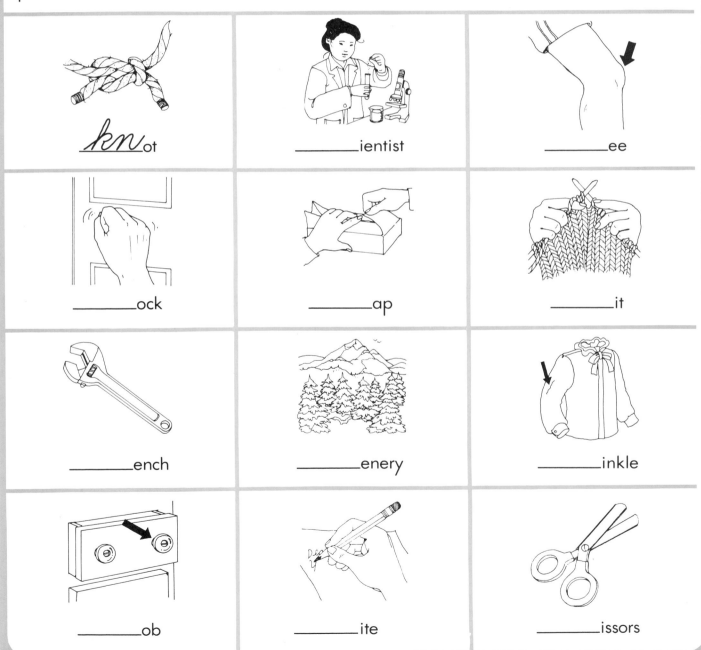

_kn_ot   _____ientist   _____ee

_____ock   _____ap   _____it

_____ench   _____enery   _____inkle

_____ob   _____ite   _____issors

Silent Consonants: KN, WR, and SC

Name _____

Read each sentence and the words beside it. Write the word that makes sense in each sentence.

1.	I left my _science_ book lying on the kitchen table.	science scene scent
2.	What kind of _____ is good for cutting apples?	know knife knee
3.	Who will be acting in the _____ that takes place in the garden?	scissors science scene
4.	A _____ made of pine cones hangs on the front door.	wrote wren wreath
5.	The bird in that tree is a _____.	write wren wreath
6.	Please bring paper, pens, and _____ to art class.	scent scissors science
7.	You will need to bring yellow yarn to the first _____ class.	kneeling knitting knocking
8.	Can we _____ something as big as a bicycle?	wrap wrong wren
9.	The people in the front row will _____ for the picture.	knew kneel know
10.	Do you _____ how many people plan to come to the party?	know knit knock

Words containing silent consonants in context: kn, wr, sc

Silent Consonants: *KN, WR,* and *SC*

Name _____

Read each set of sentences and its list of words. Write the word from the list that makes sense in each sentence.

1. Arthur helped his brother get the ___*knot*___ out of his shoelace.

2. When I finish _____ this box, we can go to the party.

3. My father _____ your mother when they were both children.

4. The _____ won a prize for her work.

5. I am afraid that I'll _____ my costume if I sit down.

6. Are those _____ sharp enough to cut this heavy paper?

knew

wrinkle

knot

scissors

wrong

wrapping

scientist

knowing

1. Was your mom able to put a new _____ on the door?

2. Is that a new watch I see on your _____?

3. Last week I bought a pair of _____ socks to go with my new skirt.

4. I have always liked smelling the _____ of roses.

5. Jennifer thought she heard a _____ at the door.

6. Did Cathy see the second _____ of the play?

scene

wrench

knob

knock

wrist

knee

wrong

scent

Silent Consonants: CK, MB, and GH

Name _____

In some words, two consonants together stand for one sound. The letters **ck** usually stand for the sound of **k,** as in **duck.** The letters **mb** usually stand for the sound of **m,** as in **lamb.** The letters **gh** are usually silent, as in **night.**

du**ck**
la**mb**
ni**gh**t

Read the list of words below. Then look at the pictures. Write a word from the list that tells about each picture.

truck	eight	comb	climb	block
brick	light	clock	thumb	

climb

_____

_____

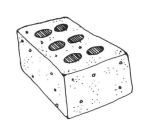

_____

_____

_____

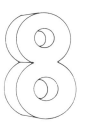

_____

_____

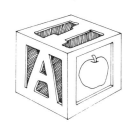

_____

Symbol-sound association of words containing silent consonants: *ck, mb, gh*

Silent Consonants: CK, MB, and GH

Name _____

Read each sentence and the words beside it. Write the word that makes sense in each sentence.

1. The little _*chicks*_ followed their mother.

   sticks
   chicks
   thick

2. My teacher _____ Allen how to play the drums.

   eight
   taught
   sight

3. Andrew will _____ his hair before his picture is taken.

   comb
   climb
   thumb

4. How many times can you run around the _____?

   pack
   track
   back

5. Our family _____ take a trip this summer.

   might
   sight
   right

6. Before the grass is cut, we must walk around the yard and pick up each _____.

   thick
   stick
   lick

7. Each fire fighter must _____ the ladder.

   thumb
   climb
   comb

8. We ate dinner on our plane _____ to the city.

   bright
   fright
   flight

9. The children have fun with these building _____.

   blocks
   socks
   locks

10. Did you hurt your _____ with the hammer?

    climb
    thumb
    comb

Name _____

Read each set of sentences and its list of words. Write the word from the list that makes sense in each sentence.

1. I was able to hold a ____*lamb*____ when I visited the zoo.

2. The new house is made of _____.

3. The little child covered with mud was quite a

    _____.

4. Do I have a hole in the toe of my _____?

5. Are you seven or _____ years old?

6. Jess plans on _____ that mountain.

7. Is the sun always so _____ in this window?

8. The dump _____ can carry a heavy load.

bright

sock

night

truck

lamb

thumb

eight

climbing

sight

bricks

1. In the winter, the birds eat the bread _____ we give them.

2. He was surprised when he _____ the ball.

3. We cannot ride our bicycles until it is _____ outside.

4. The gift was a brush and _____ set.

5. How _____ is the new downtown building?

6. Did you _____ to see that the lights are off?

7. We heard them _____ when the race was over.

comb

light

check

block

high

crumbs

sigh

climb

caught

Words containing silent consonants in context: *ck, mb, gh*

Silent Consonants

Name _____

Read each clue. Write **kn, wr, sc, ck, mb,** or **gh** to complete the word that matches the clue.

1. a time to sleep   ni_*gh*_t

2. painted scenes used in a play   _____enery

3. the flying of a plane or a jet   fli_____t

4. to make something with yarn   _____it

5. the part of the arm near the hand   _____ist

6. something used to make hair smooth   co_____

7. a baby sheep   la_____

8. the middle part of the leg   _____ee

9. a stone   ro_____

10. to put words down on paper   _____ite

11. not low   hi_____

12. something you do to get into a tree   cli_____

13. something a train moves on   tra_____

14. a tool used to tighten nuts and bolts   _____ench

15. the smell of something   _____ent

Silent Consonants

Name _____

Read the list of words below. Then read the sentences that follow. Write the word from the list that makes sense in each sentence.

crumbs	lock	knob	wrinkle	knock	science	wrap
quick	eight	scene	taught	thumb	straight	knew

1. If you ___*knock*___ three times, we'll let you into the clubhouse.

2. She twisted the _____ to turn on the television.

3. Danny painted a beautiful _____ of the mountains.

4. If we are _____, we can catch the morning train.

5. Aunt Joyce knew we had been eating because there were

    _____ on the table.

6. Be careful not to _____ your new shirt.

7. The children learned about plants in _____ class.

8. The holes in the scissors are for your finger and your _____.

9. Chee _____ his little sister how to tie her shoes.

10. What should Cindy use to _____ the food for our lunches?

11. This bicycle path goes _____ through the city.

12. So far, we have only _____ persons playing on our team.

13. Be sure to _____ the car door before you go shopping.

14. I _____ you would like reading that book.

Assessment of words containing silent consonants: *kn, wr, sc, ck, mb, gh*

Vowel Pairs: *AI*, *AY*, and *EI*

Name _____

In some words, two vowels together stand for one vowel sound. The letters **ai** and **ay** usually stand for the long-**a** sound, as in **train** and **hay.** The letters **ei** sometimes stand for the long-**a** sound, as in **eight.**

tr**ai**n
h**ay**
eight

Read the words and look at the pictures. Circle the word that tells about each picture.

sail (train) say tray	tray chain train chair	say sail stay sprain
braid trail brain tray	drain playground paint daisy	hay chain hair claim
wail stay weigh sail	sail say stay sleigh	fail vein faint veil
sprain stay spray stain	pay pail paint play	weight eight sleigh weigh

Vowel Pairs: *AI, AY,* and *EI*

Name _____

Read each sentence and words beside it. Write the word that makes sense in each sentence.

1. How long must we wait for the afternoon __*train*__ ?

   tray
   tail
   train

2. What kind of _____ do trains and planes carry?

   reigns
   freight
   sleigh

3. Can you teach me how to _____ my hair?

   braid
   chain
   grain

4. You can carry the dishes to the table on a _____.

   train
   tray
   tail

5. The nurse wrote my _____ on a chart.

   freight
   weight
   sleigh

6. Could you help me get the _____ out of the board?

   nail
   sail
   tail

7. The children liked the story about the well-known

   _____ that could fly.

   reindeer
   freight
   weight

8. Some people _____ water on their plants.

   say
   straight
   spray

9. Can you _____ at my house when your family goes away?

   stain
   stay
   sleigh

10. Do you know how to fix a bicycle _____?

    braid
    chain
    train

Words containing vowel digraphs in context: *ai, ay, ei*

Vowel Pairs: *AI, AY,* and *EI*

Name _____

Read the list of words below. Then read the sentences that follow. Write the word from the list that makes sense in each sentence.

weight	crayons	daisy	playground	aim
stay	trail	sleigh	mail	highway
neighbor	eighteen	way		

1. We count cars when our family drives on the _____*highway*_____.

2. Who will pick up your _____ at the post office when you are out of town?

3. You can score a point if you _____ the basketball at the rim.

4. Growing flowers is something my _____ does well.

5. If you walk on this dusty _____, you will come to Oak Lake.

6. Where will you _____ when you go on your trip to the city?

7. When it snows, Mrs. Bobbitt takes children on _____ rides through the woods.

8. You can find scissors, paper, and many _____ in my desk.

9. If you want to play kickball, meet on the school _____.

10. There are _____ boys and girls in that club.

11. Yoko put a _____ in her hair.

12. Which _____ should I turn when I get to the school?

13. As I grow taller, I will gain _____.

Words containing vowel digraphs in context: *ai, ay, ei*

Vowel Pairs: *EE, EA, OA,* and *OW*

Name _____

In some words, two vowels together stand for one vowel sound. The letters **ee** usually stand for the long-**e** sound, as in **bee.** The letters **ea** can stand for the long-**e** sound, as in **bean** or the short-**e** sound, as in **bread.** The letters **oa** and **ow** often stand for the long-**o** sound, as in **coat** and **window.**

b**ee**
b**ea**n
br**ea**d
c**oa**t
wind**ow**

Read the words and name the pictures. Circle the word that names each picture.

beak (bee) bow boat	green goat grow groan	bowl bread boat beach
seek sneak snow seat	head heat heel heavy	loaf leaf lean low
sheep shadow show sheet	bee beak bread beach	boat beat bean bowl
three thread throat throw	row read roast road	tea teeth tree treat

Symbol-sound association of words containing vowel digraphs: *ee, ea, oa, ow*

Vowel Pairs: *EE, EA, OA,* and *OW*

Name _____

Read each sentence and the words beside it. Write the word that makes sense in each sentence.

1.	Do you know how to tie a _____ *bow* _____?	bow beak bee
2.	I fixed the _____ of my bicycle.	wheat wheel week
3.	Would you like some butter or jelly on your _____?	toast team teeth
4.	You may have some eggs for _____.	bread breakfast breath
5.	Our basketball _____ works hard when it plays.	team tow teen
6.	Today we'll have _____ and crackers for our snack.	cheek cheese cheap
7.	The school nurse says I am very _____.	heats healthy heel
8.	That dish can be cleaned with _____ and water.	soap seed seal
9.	When my uncle sees me he always says, "My, how you've _____."	grown green greet
10.	We will go swimming at the _____ behind our neighbor's house.	beak beach been

Vowel Pairs: *EE, EA, OA,* and *OW*

Name _____

Read the list of words below. Then read the sentences that follow. Write the word from the list that makes sense in each sentence.

need	teeth	heavy	show	bowl
reach	steep	float	goat	teacher
grow	meant	feather	roast	

1. Jane will be happy to ___*show*___ you her drawing.

2. We had fun feeding the playful _____ at the zoo.

3. The chart on the classroom wall was made by the _____.

4. We were careful when we climbed the _____ hill.

5. The basket of apples was too _____ for me to carry.

6. Justin _____ to call you this morning.

7. My little sister tried to _____ the books on the highest shelf.

8. When we were in the swimming pool, my dad showed me how to

   _____.

9. The dentist checks my _____ twice a year.

10. Will I _____ eggs to make the muffins?

11. Let's put the popcorn in this yellow _____.

12. This daisy will _____ to be as tall as the fence.

13. I found a bird's _____ on the beach.

14. How long will it take to _____ the meat in this oven?

Words containing vowel digraphs in context: *ee, ea, oa, ow*

Vowel Pairs: *EE, EA, OA,* and *OW*

Name _____

Read each sentence and look at the vowel pairs beside it. Write one of the vowel pairs to complete the unfinished word in each sentence. The word you form must make sense in the sentence.

1. Put on your heavy c_*oa*_t before we go outside.   oa, ea

2. I can hear the wind bl_____ing.   ee, ow

3. Let's walk on this winding r_____d that leads to the barn.   oa, ee

4. We will give the horse a tr_____t.   ea, ow

5. The horse likes to eat _____ts from our hands.   ea, oa

6. Don't you think its fun to _____n a horse?   ow, ee

---

1. It's always pl_____sant to think about a summer trip.   oa, ea

2. I like to dr_____m about the many places I want to visit.   ea, ow

3. Sometime I'd like to take a long b_____t trip so I could see the sights.   ea, oa

4. I have always m_____nt to plan a train trip to the West.   ow, ea

5. The train I want to ride would have a place for me to sl_____p.   ee, ow

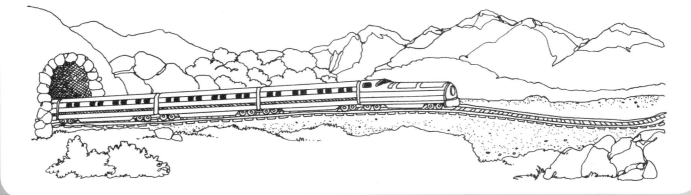

Vowel Pairs: *OO*, *AU*, *AW*, and *EW*

Name _____

In some words, two vowels together stand for one sound. The letters **oo** can stand for the sound you hear in the middle of **moon** or **book**. The letters **au** usually stand for the sound you hear at the beginning of **auto**. The letters **aw** usually stand for the sound you hear at the end of **saw**. The letters **ew** usually stand for the sound you hear in the middle of **news**.

m**oo**n
b**oo**k
auto
s**aw**
n**ew**s

Read the words and look at the pictures. Circle the word that tells about each picture.

(book) boot blew broom	screw school straw spoon	faucet few fault flew
droop draw dew dawn	claw jaw jewel chew	hook haul hoop hood
food fool flew foot	lawn look launch law	pool straw paw spoon
saw screw soon straw	blew boot book brook	noon blew news book

Symbol-sound association of vowel digraphs: *oo, au, aw, ew*

Vowel Pairs: OO, AU, AW, and EW

<u>Name</u>

Read each sentence and the words beside it. Write the word that makes sense in each sentence.

1. The light of the ___*moon*___ was bright last night.

    mew
    moon
    moose

2. I believe there are a _____ tickets left for the show.

    fawn
    few
    fault

3. Patrick _____ in the rain and waited for the bus.

    spoon
    scoop
    stood

4. We will get up at _____ to catch the early morning train.

    dawn
    dew
    draw

5. What kind of _____ should we make for the meat?

    sauce
    screw
    straw

6. Colleen _____ a picture of the snowy mountains.

    dew
    drew
    droop

7. Does that _____ crow every morning?

    raccoon
    spoon
    rooster

8. The new speed _____ helps keep the highways safe.

    look
    launch
    law

9. Marty hit a fly ball, and Benny _____ it.

    caught
    claw
    cause

10. Richard _____ the coins out of his piggy bank.

    shook
    straw
    sauce

Vowel Pairs: OO, AU, AW, and EW

Name _____

Read the list of words below. Then read the sentences that follow. Write the word from the list that makes sense in each sentence.

cause	look	yawn	flew	daughter
hawk	few	kangaroo	hook	taught
tooth	drawings	spoon	grew	

1. The baby needs a _____*spoon*_____ for the food.

2. His little sister just lost a front _____.

3. I _____ when I get up too early in the morning.

4. Martin likes to make _____ of birds and flowers.

5. Please hang your coat on the _____ behind the door.

6. Can you tell me if that bird is a _____?

7. The princess is the _____ of the queen.

8. My aunt will _____ for a new car today.

9. My teacher _____ me how to add numbers.

10. Do you have a _____ minutes to listen to my tape?

11. When my family visited the zoo, my brother wanted to see a baby

    _____ in its mother's pouch.

12. Do the fire fighters know the _____ of the fire?

13. A hot-air balloon _____ over the fairgrounds this morning.

14. The farmers _____ more corn this year than last.

Words containing vowel digraphs in context: *oo, au, aw, ew*

Vowel Pairs: *OO, AU, AW,* and *EW*

Name _____

Read each sentence and look at the vowel pairs beside it. Write one of the vowel pairs to complete the unfinished word in each sentence. The word you form must make sense in the sentence.

1. There is much to do after sch_*oo*_l.   oo, au

2. You may plan to play baseball on the front l_____n.   aw, ew

3. The swimming p_____l is open.   oo, au

4. You can check out a b_____k from the library.   oo, aw

5. You'll need to p_____se and think about what you'd like to do.   au, oo

---

1. One day we got up at d_____n.   aw, oo

2. A f_____ of us quickly got dressed.   aw, ew

3. We had planned a walk in the w_____ds.   oo, au

4. Our leader had t_____ght us about animal tracks.   oo, au

5. Before long, Danny s_____ some small tracks.   oo, aw

6. We were following a family of racc_____ns.   au, oo

Vowel Pairs

Name _____

Read the list of words below. Then read the sentences that follow. Write the word from the list that makes sense in each sentence.

bread	train	stay	speak	steep	soon	keep
book	draw	few	jewel	own	road	drew

1. I would like to make some ___*bread*___ for my neighbor.

2. Can you _____ here awhile and help me bake a loaf?

3. I need a map that shows the _____ where the shops are.

4. Please _____ the map with a marker on this sheet of paper.

5. Will you _____ these tickets for me until I'm ready to go?

6. I will be taking a _____ ride into the city to see your daughter.

7. Nancy got a _____ from the library today.

8. Someday she would like to have her _____ set of books.

9. My aunt and uncle have a _____ horses and cows.

10. They will also have sheep at their ranch _____.

11. Andrew _____ a picture of a fancy crown.

12. A beautiful _____ was in the center of the crown.

13. Are you able to _____ to the group at this week's meeting?

14. We would like to hear about the _____ mountain you climbed.

Vowel Pairs: *IE*

Name _____

Tie has the long-**i** sound spelled by the letters **ie**. Shield has the long-**e** sound spelled by the letters **ie**.

tie   **sh**i**e**ld

Read the words and look at the pictures. Circle the word that tells about each picture.

(tie) lie		die pie		lie necktie	
field lie	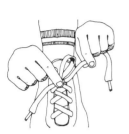	niece movie		chief thief	
field movie		die chief		piece die	
cookie tie		piece pie		field shield	

Vowel Pairs: *IE*

Name _____

Read the list of words. Notice the sound that **ie** stands for in each word. Then write each word under the correct heading.

tie   **shield**

field	lie	niece	thief
necktie	pie	die	movie

Long i as in tie

necktie

_____

_____

_____

Long e as in shield

_____

_____

_____

_____

Read the sentences. Complete each sentence by writing a word from the exercise above. The word you write must make sense in the sentence.

1. His _necktie_ matched the color of his jacket.

2. We like to pick wild flowers from the _____ near our home.

3. Would you like to _____ down and rest?

4. Her family watched an exciting _____ about runners.

5. What made that plant _____?

6. My _____ has a beautiful smile.

7. The _____ had taken the important papers.

Symbol-sound association of words containing *ie*; Words containing *ie* in context

Vowel Pairs: *IE*

Name _____

Read the sentences and the list of words. Write the word from the list that makes sense in each sentence.

tie   **shield**

1. Mindy will _____*tie*_____ string around the box.

2. I would like to be the _____ of the fire fighters.

3. I _____ you can run the race faster than you ever have before.

4. Should my dad wear a _____ tonight?

5. The grass will _____ if it doesn't get enough water.

6. Have you ever told a _____?

7. May I have another _____ of paper?

8. The teacher showed a _____ after we talked about the city.

9. The police are looking for the _____ who ran out of the bank with the money.

10. I have been an aunt since my _____ Kris was born.

11. The team can play softball in that _____.

12. Each knight in the painting is holding a heavy

_____.

chief

shield

die

piece

niece

necktie

thief

lie

field

believe

movie

tie

Vowel Pairs: OU

Name _____

In some words, two vowels together stand for one vowel sound. The letters **ou** can stand for the vowel sounds you hear in **soup** and **should.**

s**ou**p
sh**ou**ld

Read the list of words. Notice the sound that **ou** stands for in each word. Write each word under the correct heading.

group	wouldn't	could	through	coupon
would	shouldn't	youth	couldn't	you

ou as in **soup**   **ou** as in **should**

_____ *group* _____   _____

_____   _____

_____   _____

_____   _____

Read the sentences and the word choices. Circle the word that makes sense in each sentence.

1. Grandmother told me I (through, (should)) remember to wear my coat.

2. (Wouldn't, Youth) it be nice to have a picture of that sunset?

3. We save money by using (should, coupons) when we shop.

4. A (group, couldn't) of six children will play on each team.

5. Our teacher told us we (coupon, could) write a story.

6. What kind of (should, soup) do I smell cooking?

7. We will hike over the hill and (would, through) the woods.

Symbol-sound association of words containing *ou*; Words containing *ou* in context

Vowel Pairs: *OU*

Name _____

touch
doughnut

In some words, two vowels together stand for one vowel sound. The letters **ou** can stand for the vowel sounds you hear in **touch** and **doughnut**.

Read the list of words. Notice the sound that **ou** stands for in each word. Write each word under the correct heading.

double	couple	dough	southern	shoulder
enough	although	young	though	

ou as in touch

double

_____

_____

_____

_____

ou as in doughnut

_____

_____

_____

Read the sentences and the word choices. Circle the word that makes sense in each sentence.

1. Have you ever tasted bread (dough, double) like this?

2. Debbie knows how to make whole wheat (double, doughnuts).

3. Would you like to visit my uncle in the (country, couple)?

4. Jennie's (cousin, though) can make flutes out of wood.

5. The player who made a (touchdown, through) jumped up and down.

6. I put the backpack over my (southern, shoulder).

7. Do you have (enough, although) wood to build a fire?

Vowel Pairs: *OU*

Name _____

Read the story. Circle each word that contains **ou.** Then answer the questions that follow. There are twenty-three words that contain **ou.**

(Though) we had never done it before, our youth group planned to make bread. We should have started with something easy, but we like bread! We went through the food store with many coupons, buying enough for an army.

Jan wanted us to get double of everything on our list. Doug had to carry a large bag of flour over his shoulder. The shopkeeper said it looked as if we were going to open a shop with all of the bread we planned to make.

The next day we all met at the home of Jan's cousin. Our plan was to first mix a little bit of the dough. We didn't have any trouble. Before long, we had baked a beautiful loaf of bread. We spent the rest of the day baking bread. By the time we were through, we had enough for each of us to take a loaf home.

I shared my bread with my family. My dad said, "The group you belong to is young, but they surely know how to bake." He should know. He ate five pieces!

Use the story to answer the questions.

1. What word from the first paragraph rhymes with **dough?** ___*though*___

2. What kind of group baked the bread? _____

3. What did the group take to the store in order to save money? _____

4. What word from the second paragraph means "twice as much"? _____

5. How did Doug carry the flour? _____

6. What word from the third paragraph means "finished"? _____

Identifying words containing *ou*; Words containing *ou* in context

Vowel Pairs

Name _____

Read the list of words below. Then read the sentences that follow. Write the word from the list that makes sense in each sentence.

necktie	field	dough	would	should
chief	enough	tie	believe	
route	touch	movie	through	

1. I have never worn a ___*necktie*___ before.

2. Will you show me how to _____ it?

3. What _____ I do without your help?

4. We can make this _____ into bread or rolls.

5. There may be _____ of the mix to make both.

6. Let's taste the bread as soon as we're _____.

7. This is the _____ shown on the map that we should follow.

8. It will take us past a _____ of corn.

9. Can you _____ that covered wagons once used this road?

10. Would you and your brother like to see a good _____?

11. The show is about a well-known Indian _____.

12. The zoo worker said that some snakes _____ be fed every day.

13. She asked us if we'd like to _____ the skin of a snake.

Name _____

When **y** comes at the end of a word that has no other vowel, the **y** usually stands for the long-**i** sound as in **fly.** When **y** comes at the end of a word that has another vowel, the **y** usually stands for the long-**e** sound as in **pony.**

fl**y**   pon**y**

Read the words and look at the pictures. Circle the word that tells about each picture.

fly (jelly)	spy / puppy	carry / cry
dry / daisy	fly / funny	fry / forty
sky / snowy	try / rainy	funny / fry
daisy / dry	silly / sky	rocky / cry

Symbol-sound association of words containing *y* as a vowel

Two Sounds of Y

Name _____

Read the words below. Write **long e** or **long i** next to each word to show the sound that **y** stands for.

fl**y**   pon**y**

1. fly   *long i*

2. angry   _____

3. sixty   _____

4. why   _____

5. dry   _____

6. thirsty   _____

7. stormy   _____

8. shy   _____

9. lucky   _____

10. fry   _____

11. empty   _____

12. cry   _____

Read the sentences and the word choices. Circle the word that makes sense in each sentence.

1. Tommy will (try, fry) to answer each of your questions.

2. Can you get me a (carry, copy) of the story you read to us today?

3. We can go sled riding on the first (sixty, snowy) day.

4. When I learned that my best friend was moving, I began to (dry, cry).

5. Should we buy a pack of twenty or (rainy, forty) paper plates for the party?

6. On the day we began our trip there wasn't a cloud in the (shy, sky).

7. Are those math books too (heavy, healthy) for you to carry?

8. I'd like to know (shy, why) the date of the football game was changed.

Identifying vowel sounds of y; Words containing y as a vowel in context

Two Sounds of Y

Name _____

Read the list of words. Notice the sound that **y** stands for in each word. Write each word under the correct heading.

fl**y**   pon**y**

| try | sky | sixty | stormy | fry |
| cry | penny | rocky | shiny | shy |

Long **i** as in **fly**

try

_____

_____

_____

_____

Long **e** as in **pony**

_____

_____

_____

_____

_____

Read the sentences. Complete each sentence by writing a word from the exercise above. The word you write must make sense in the sentence.

1. Would you like to ____*try*____ to fly my new kite?

2. We climbed up the steep, _____ hillside.

3. Will that school bus hold more than _____ children?

4. Have you ever tried to count each star in the _____?

5. Uncle Richard can bake or _____ the fish in a pan for you.

6. Aunt Janie's new _____ bicycle is silver.

Symbol-sound association of words containing *y* as a vowel; Words containing *y* as a vowel in context

Vowel Pairs and Sounds of Y

Name _____

Read the list of words below. Then read the sentences that follow. Write the word from the list that makes sense in each sentence.

try	taught	weight	raccoon	healthy
field	trail	cousin	cheese	straw
toast	chew	window	through	

1. We should _____*try*_____ to get together to play basketball.

2. I would like two eggs and some _____ with jam this morning.

3. The farmer carried a bale of _____ into the barn.

4. The nurse always checks the baby's _____ on the scales.

5. Dennis _____ us how to use a rowboat.

6. What kind of _____ should I put on this sandwich?

7. Mandy's puppy likes to _____ toy bones.

8. We can fly kites from the grassy _____.

9. Eating good food helps you stay _____.

10. I wish my _____ could go shopping with us.

11. Every year the hiking _____ is used by many people.

12. I never rode _____ a tunnel.

13. If you look out this _____, you can see the lights of the city.

14. Did you see that _____ walking on our picnic table?

City Workers

Many people in the city work to help us. They do things for us that we cannot do for ourselves.

Police

Police officers help us in many ways. They help people cross the street safely. They help little children find their way if they are lost. They find people who break the law. They make our cities safe to live in.

Mail Carriers

Mail carriers bring letters and newspapers to people's homes. They also bring books, toys, and clothes that we have sent away for. They do their work in sun, snow, rain, or wind.

Fire Fighters

Fire fighters are ready at all times to fight fires. They put out fires in homes and other buildings. They save people's lives. They go to schools to teach children about fire safety.

1. Check the answer that tells the main idea.

   _____ people who help us

   _____ what people can do to help the police

   _____ how to fight fires

2. Write two things that fire fighters do.

   _____

   _____

Application of reading and comprehension skills in a social studies context

Name _____

3. Write the name of the worker under each picture.

_____   _____   _____

4. In what way are a police officer and a fire fighter the same?

_____

5. Tell how your life might be different without one of these city workers.

         police   mail carriers   fire fighters

_____

_____

_____

6. Choose one of these city workers. Tell how this person helps people in the city.

    bus driver   mayor   lifeguard   street cleaner

_____

_____

_____

Application of thinking and writing skills in a social studies context

Consonant Pairs

Name _____

Two consonants together can stand for one sound. Some consonants that stand for one sound are **sh, ch, th,** and **wh.** At the beginning of some words, three consonants together stand for a special sound as in **three.**

shoe　　　　**wh**eel
chair　　　　**thr**ee
thin

Name the pictures. Write the letters that stand for the beginning sound in each picture name.

*thr*___ead	_____ovel	_____irteen
		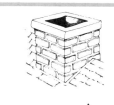
_____ain	_____eel	_____imney

Read the sentences. Complete the unfinished word in each sentence by writing the missing letters. Choose from the following consonant pairs: **sh, ch, th, wh, thr.** You may use a consonant pair more than once.

1. My dog looks like a puppy, but he is ___*thr*___ee years old.

2. When he was a puppy, he would drag my old _____ite shirt around.

3. Sometimes he would hide it under a _____air.

4. Do you know that he is still afraid of his own _____adow?

5. I like to _____ow a ball for him to catch.

6. I _____ink my dog is great fun to watch!

Sound-symbol association of words containing initial consonant digraphs; Words containing initial consonant digraphs in context: *sh, ch, th, wh, thr*

Consonant Pairs

Name _____

Read each sentence and the words beside it. Write the word that makes sense in each sentence.

1. If you get some ___*thread*___ , I will fix your coat.

cheese
thread
shed

2. I always lay my glasses on this _____.

three
shelf
check

3. In art class, we form clay into many different _____.

shapes
change
thanks

4. The police believe that a _____ tried to break into the bank.

thief
whip
chin

5. I will read my book _____ you talk to the man who works in the children's library.

child
while
shield

6. Are there any sea animals bigger than a _____?

chain
shake
whale

7. Is there a _____ that you'll be able to go swimming with me?

shark
than
chance

8. The queen sat on a _____ to receive her crown.

shook
throne
choke

9. Our group would like to _____ you for your help with the play.

thank
chain
shadow

10. Before we build a fire, let's have the _____ cleaned.

thirteen
chimney
whistle

Ending Consonant Pairs

Name _____

At the end of a word, two or three consonants together can stand for one sound. Some consonants that stand for one sound are **sh, ch, tch, th,** and **ng.**

wi**sh**	wi**th**
ea**ch**	ri**ng**
ca**tch**	

Name the pictures. Write the letters that stand for the ending sound in each picture name.

pea_*ch*_____

wa_____

bru_____

tee_____

ben_____

stri_____

Read the sentences. Complete the unfinished word in each sentence by writing the letters that stand for the ending sound. Choose from the following consonant pairs: **sh, ch, tch, th, ng.** You may use a consonant pair more than once. The word you form must make sense in the sentence.

1. Please come alo_*ng*_____ with Callie and me.

2. Bo_____ of us would like you to join the baseball team.

3. Today the coach will tea_____ us how to pitch.

4. Next week we will learn more about how to ca_____ the ball.

5. We'll have to ru_____ if we want to be at the field on time.

Sound-symbol association of words containing final consonant digraphs; Words containing final consonant digraphs in context: *sh, ch, tch, th, ng*

Ending Consonant Pairs

Name _____

Read each sentence and the words beside it. Write the word that makes sense in each sentence.

1. The band will ___*march*___ onto the field and play the school song.

match
math
march

2. This morning we bought enough _____ for two kites.

scratch
splash
string

3. A large _____ was broken off our elm tree during the storm.

both
brush
branch

4. The picture will turn out better if you use a _____ on your camera.

flash
splash
crash

5. How many _____ does the baby have now?

teach
teeth
leash

6. When the bell _____, the children hurried from the playground to the classroom.

ranch
rash
rang

7. Our sleds made a _____ through the snowy woods.

path
patch
peach

8. The _____ on this lamp is broken.

switch
such
swing

9. The kitten didn't mean to _____ you.

spring
scratch
sang

10. When I visit my cousins' farm, I like to _____ the horses.

branch
booth
brush

Words containing final consonant digraphs in context: *sh, ch, tch, th, ng*

Consonant Pairs

Name _____

The letters **gh** sometimes stand for the sound of **f,** as in lau**gh**. The letters **ph** usually stand for the sound of **f,** as in ele**ph**ant.

lau**gh**   ele**ph**ant

Read the words and look at the pictures. Circle the word that tells about each picture.

(photo)

tough

alphabet

laughing

phone

cough

tough

telephone

laugh

photo

enough

elephant

Read the sentences and the word choices. Circle the word that makes sense in each sentence.

1. Will you answer the (telephone, rough) while I am reading?

2. When we drive our car over the (phone, rough) road, we bounce on the seats.

3. Sammy likes to take (laugh, photos) when he's on a trip.

4. When you visited the zoo, did you see the baby (elephant, rough)?

5. The meat is too (phone, tough) to cut with this knife.

6. Does Sandy have (enough, telephone) paper for art class?

7. Rosa makes faces to make the baby (laugh, photo).

Symbol-sound association of words containing consonant digraphs;
Words containing consonant digraphs in context: *gh, ph*

Consonant Pairs

Name _____

Read the list of words below. Then read the sentences that follow. Write the word from the list that makes sense in each sentence.

tough	elephant	telephone	alphabet
laugh	enough	rough	nephew
microphone	rougher	photograph	laughing

1. You may want to use a _microphone_ when you speak to large groups.

2. Will Brad have _____ time to visit us this week?

3. Dad is teaching Sue the letters of the _____.

4. I know you'll _____ when you read this funny story.

5. Because the wood of the chair is _____, we'll use sandpaper to make it smooth.

6. My sister is my aunt's niece, and my brother is her

   _____.

7. The children were _____ at the circus clown.

8. I am sorry that the meat I cooked is so _____.

9. This road is _____ than it was last winter.

10. I can't hear the _____ ringing when I'm working outside.

11. Ann wants to give me a _____ of her cats.

12. Val has always wanted to feed peanuts to an _____.

Words containing *gh* and *ph* in context

Consonant Pairs

Name _____

Read the list of words below. Then read the clues that follow. Write the word from the list that matches each clue.

rough   tough   laugh   telephone   photo
nephew   enough   alphabet   elephant

1. not smooth   *rough*

2. what you do when you think something is funny _____

3. a boy who has an aunt or uncle   _____

4. starts with **a, b, c**   _____

5. as much as is needed   _____

6. something you can use to talk with another person _____

7. hard to chew or cut   _____

8. a picture that is taken with a camera   _____

9. a large circus animal   _____

Read the sentences and the word choices. Circle the word that makes sense in each sentence.

1. Her little sister knows the letters of the (alphabet, elephant).

2. Please answer the (tough, telephone) for me.

3. The bark of that tree feels very (rough, laugh).

4. I would like to see the (enough, photos) you took with your camera.

5. The jokes in your book made me (nephew, laugh).

Consonant Pairs

Name _____

Read each clue. Write **sh, ch, wh, ng,** or **gh** to complete the word that matches the clue.

1. a food made from milk _____*ch*_____eese

2. something you blow into that makes a high noise _____istle

3. a tool used for digging _____ovel

4. two pieces of bread with meat between them sandwi_____

5. a playground toy you can sit on swi_____

6. hard to cut tou_____

7. something you make when you jump into water spla_____

Read each clue. Write **th, ph, thr,** or **tch** to complete the word that matches the clue.

1. something that can feel sore when you have a cold _____*thr*_____oat

2. a number greater than two _____ee

3. a picture taken with a camera _____oto

4. a part of your hand _____umb

5. a piece of cloth that covers a hole in a piece of clothing pa_____

6. something that is used to make clothes clo_____

7. something used to light a candle ma_____

Review of words containing initial and final consonant digraphs

Consonant Pairs

Name _____

Read each set of sentences and its list of words. Write the word from the list that makes sense in each sentence.

1. My family likes to _____*watch*_____ parades.

2. We always go early so that we can sit on a _____.

3. The last parade we saw had _____ marching bands.

4. I clapped as I saw each one _____ by.

5. When I knew the tunes, I would _____ along.

6. I was surprised to see a float being pulled by an

    _____.

7. If I were in a parade, the children would

    _____ at my funny clown costume.

march
laugh
thumb
watch
elephant
bench
sing
thirty
catch

---

1. I _____ this room looked nicer.

2. I wonder if I should paint the walls _____.

3. Should I keep _____ the lamp and the basket on that table?

4. Shall I put two or _____ pictures on this wall?

5. Where should I hang this _____ for my books?

6. Please tell me what you _____ about this chair.

7. Did I hear you say, "Don't _____ a thing"?

shelf
both
wish
whisper
three
white
shake
change
think

Assessment of words containing initial and final consonant digraphs in context

Vowels With R

Name _____

When a vowel is followed by the letter **r,** the vowel stands for a special sound that is neither long nor short. For example, **ar** stands for the sound you hear in **jar; er, ir,** and **ur** stand for the sounds you hear in **fern, bird,** and **burn; or** stands for the sound you hear in **horn.**

j**ar**	h**or**n
f**er**n	b**ur**n
b**ir**d	

Name the pictures and read the sentences. Circle the word in each sentence that has the same vowel sound as the picture name.

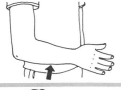
1. This spring we'll be planting corn in our (garden.)

2. Amy's brother is too short to see out the car window.

3. I would like to knit a scarf that will match the color of this skirt.

4. The kitten likes to curl up and sleep on the front porch.

5. My friends and I put on a make-believe circus in the park.

6. An artist could turn this white wall into a beautiful picture.

7. If you turn down this path, you will see a pine forest.

Vowels With *R*

Name _____

Read the list of words below. Then read the questions that follow. Write the word from the list that answers each question.

turkey	porch	nurse	storm	stars
scarf	dirt	forest	slippers	herd
purple	thirty	card	ladder	

1. What is a large bird? _*turkey*_

2. In what is a seed planted? _____

3. What brings snow or rain? _____

4. What can you sign and send in the mail? _____

5. What can be worn on your feet? _____

6. What can you wear to keep your head or neck

   warm? _____

7. Who helps care for people who are ill? _____

8. What can you use to climb to high places? _____

9. What has many trees? _____

10. What is a group of cows called? _____

11. What can be seen in the sky at night? _____

12. What number comes after twenty-nine? _____

13. What is a color? _____

14. What can be on the front of a house? _____

Words containing *r*-controlled vowels in context

Vowels With *R*

Name _____

Read the sentences and the word choices. Circle the word that makes sense in each sentence.

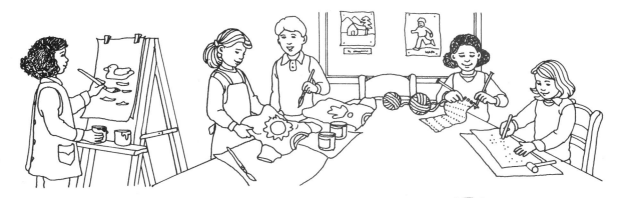

1. I go to the craft center with my friends each Saturday ((morning,) market).

2. The (teachers, torch) show us a different craft every week.

3. One time, we made little (lanterns, large) out of tin.

4. Another time, I used a new kind of paint to color a white (shirt, sharp).

5. I have made a scarf out of yarn and a belt out of (ladder, leather).

6. Sometimes I make mistakes, but most of my things (torn, turn) out all right.

7. My work at the center makes me want to become an (artist, other).

---

1. Last night's storm made a mess of our (yard, yarn).

2. Now we must try to save the plants in our (germ, garden).

3. Our tall green corn plants are now lying in the (dirt, dart).

4. I'll use a broom to sweep the front (perch, porch).

5. My older brother and my (sister, squirrel) will get the tree branches off the roof.

6. We are lucky that the storm did not (her, hurt) the apple tree we just planted.

7. I hope the wind doesn't blow so (hard, horn) in the next storm.

Words containing *r*-controlled vowels in context

Vowels With *R*

Name _____

Read each sentence and look at the letter pairs beside it. Write one of the letter pairs to complete the unfinished word in each sentence. The word you form must make sense in the sentence.

1. We planted rows of seeds in the g_*ar*_den.   ar, er

2. I like to watch the dancer t_____n when he dances on the stage.   or, ur

3. The tail of the squ_____rel is bushy.   ar, ir

4. Before it snows, we will cov_____ the plants in our garden.   or, er

5. A sales cl_____k will be able to help you find a shirt in your size.   er, or

6. We put our bikes in the shed when it began to st_____m.   ur, or

7. I feed my t_____tle once a day in the morning.   or, ur

8. There are seats for f_____ty children in the classroom.   ir, or

9. We buy our eggs and milk at a f_____m.   or, ar

10. You'll find the answ_____ to your question in this book.   or, er

11. Shane would like to try out for a p_____t in the play.   ir, ar

12. The hamm_____ hit my thumb instead of the nail.   er, ar

13. This ch_____t shows how far I have run this spring.   ar, or

14. Carla has my comb in her p_____se.   ar, ur

15. The group must form a c_____cle before the game begins.   ar, ir

Words containing *r*-controlled vowels in context

Vowels With R

Name _____

Read the sentences and the list of words. Write the word from the list that makes sense in each sentence.

1. A _____*turtle*_____ is a good pet to keep in a small home.

2. There are twelve fresh eggs in the _____.

3. The balloon made a loud noise when it _____.

4. That pile of _____ must be moved before the building begins.

5. The artist uses gold and _____ to make bracelets.

6. My baby brother is too _____ to reach the doorknob.

7. Which runner do you think will be the _____ to cross the finish line?

8. Please pass the salt and _____ shakers to me.

9. What kind of wood will _____ best in a fireplace?

10. Sometimes my dog _____ when I won't let her come outside with me.

11. Our class will hear a _____ talk about her trip to Spain.

12. My older sister lives in an _____ near our house.

13. I know spring is near when I hear the birds _____.

14. The puppy was _____ three weeks ago.

burn

first

chirp

pepper

silver

apartment

dirt

burst

speaker

born

turtle

barks

short

carton

Vowels With *R*

Name _____

Read the list of words below. Then read the sentences that follow. Write the word from the list that makes sense in each sentence.

porch	better	squirrels	thirty
hurry	alarm	slippers	birthday
parking	forget	horse	hurt

1. After school I come home and sit on the front _____ *porch* _____.

2. I like to watch the _____ run through the trees.

3. They make me _____ the cares of my day.

4. Don takes lessons to learn how to ride a _____.

5. His teacher says that Don's riding is getting _____ every week.

6. I'll be going to Kate's surprise _____ party next week.

7. The party will be held at the park behind the school _____ lot.

8. I must _____ to get to the post office.

9. The mail will be picked up there in _____ minutes.

10. I jumped out of bed when the _____ rang this morning.

11. One of my _____ fell off as I ran down the hallway.

12. I'm surprised I didn't _____ myself as I hurried through the house.

Assessment of words containing *r*-controlled vowels in context

OI, OY, OU, and OW

Name _____

The letters **oi** and **oy** stand for the vowel sounds in **coin** and **toys**. The letters **ou** and **ow** often stand for the vowel sounds you hear in **cloud** and **cow**.

coin	**clou**d
toys	**cow**

Read the list of words below. Then look at the pictures. Write a word from the list that tells about each picture.

cloud   point   frown   boy   boil   bounce

cloud

_____

_____

_____

_____

_____

Read the sentences and the word choices. Circle the word that makes sense in each sentence.

1. Last weekend my cousin and I were looking (around, allow) his basement.

2. We (foil, found) a trunk that was full of old picture books.

3. One book had a picture of a different circus (cloud, clown) on each page.

4. Another book had drawings of beautiful (flowers, found).

5. My cousin's mother told me I could have my (crowd, choice) of the old books.

6. I (join, enjoy) looking at the book about animals that I took home.

OI, OY, OU, and OW

Name _____

Read each sentence and the words beside it. Write the word that makes sense in each sentence.

1. My neighbor's little ___*boy*___ likes to ride his bicycle on the bike path.

   boil
   boy

2. My sister can name the different kinds of _____ in the sky.

   clouds
   coins

3. Every child in that family has a beautiful singing _____.

   voice
   vow

4. The _____ princess told the children a story.

   royal
   round

5. We learned that some plants can have _____ in them.

   pound
   poison

6. Rose tries to see how high the basketball will _____.

   boiling
   bounce

7. I would like to take a picture of the sand castle before the waves _____ it.

   down
   destroy

8. Is this dark _____ good for growing corn?

   scout
   soil

9. When we walked through the barn, I saw a _____ run across the floor.

   mouse
   mouth

10. The young girl _____ when she lost her balloon.

    frowned
    found

Words containing diphthongs in context: oi, oy, ou, ow

OI, OY, OU, and OW

Name _____

Read the clues and the list of words. Write the word from the list that matches each clue.

1. something that helps to keep machines running ___*oil*___

2. sounds _____

3. to yell _____

4. a large bird _____

5. a farm tool that loosens dirt _____

6. things that children play with _____

7. a group of many people _____

8. to hit with a hammer _____

9. something that water does when it is very hot _____

10. dirt _____

11. the sharp end of something _____

12. the part of the face used to smile _____

13. a very tall building _____

14. a young man _____

15. a sea animal that lives in a shell _____

pound

oil

shout

tower

plow

soil

noises

point

boy

toys

boils

crowd

mouth

owl

oyster

Words containing diphthongs: *oi, oy, ou, ow*

95

OI, OY, OU, and OW

Name _____

Read each sentence and look at the letter pairs beside it. Write one of the letter pairs to complete the unfinished word in each sentence. The word you form must make sense in the sentence.

1. I will see if Dad will all_ow_ me to take the bus.   ow, oi

2. I would like to ride to t_____n with my friend Beth.   oy, ow

3. If we go right after school, there will be no cr_____ds in the stores.   ow, oy

4. Beth knows how to get ar_____nd from one place to another.   ou, oi

5. She will help me find a t_____ for Timmy's birthday.   oy, ou

6. We will go to a shop that sells stamps and c_____ns.   ow, oi

7. Beth thinks I will enj_____ looking in the other store windows, too.   ou, oy

8. We are planning to return to Beth's h_____se before it gets dark.   oi, ou

---

1. Last spring I wanted to j_____n an outdoors club.   oi, ow

2. My friend Joy told me about being a sc_____t.   oi, ou

3. I would enj_____ being a member of the group.   oy, ou

4. Our hike up Snowball M_____ntain was one I'll never forget.   ou, oi

5. The hike back d_____n to our campsite was not easy because the mountain paths are steep.   oi, ow

6. I am pr_____d to be a part of the group.   ou, oi

Words containing diphthongs in context: *oi, oy, ou, ow*

OI, OY, OU, and OW

Name _____

Read the sentences and the word choices. Circle the word that makes sense in each sentence.

1. Flowers will grow well in this rich (sound, (soil)).

2. The singer works hard to make his (voice, choice) sound better.

3. When I went shopping, I bought eggs, milk, and a bag of (frown, flour).

4. Martha and Sandra are building a tall (tower, powder) of blocks.

5. The princess doll wears a golden (count, crown) on her head.

6. I like to (bounce, bow) the ball when I am on the school playground.

7. I have learned how to check the (out, oil) in our family car.

8. What kind of bath (toys, town) do babies like best?

9. When you are so far away, I can hear you only if you (shower, shout).

10. My dog will (ground, growl) if he hears a strange noise.

11. The scientist can check for (poisons, pound) in a plant.

12. I saw an (oil, oyster) shell when I visited the beach.

13. An older friend taught me how to (pound, powder) a nail into a board.

14. The beautiful horses belong to the queen and her (royal, voice) family.

15. The white, fluffy (clown, clouds) look pretty in the blue sky.

16. She has lived in this (town, toy) since she was a young girl.

17. A little gray (mouth, mouse) ran across the barn.

18. Put the corn into the pan after the water begins to (boil, bow).

OI, OY, OU, and OW

Name _____

Read the list of words below. Then read the sentences that follow. Write the word from the list that makes sense in each sentence.

ouch	clown	point	pound
frowning	boil	out	towel
boys	enjoy	join	choice

1. Let me know when the water in the pan starts to ___*boil*___.

2. I have more than one _____ of green beans to cook.

3. My family will _____ eating something from our garden.

4. Do you know why I am _____?

5. I just fell _____ of that small oak tree.

6. I am not hurt, but I did yell "_____" when I landed.

7. My sister has fun when she dresses up as a _____.

8. She says it's fun to make girls and _____ smile.

9. Please _____ to the row you would like to sit in.

10. Today you can have your _____ of seats.

11. Will you _____ me when I go to the beach to swim?

12. Don't forget your sunglasses and a _____.

Assessment of words containing diphthongs in context: *oi, oy, ou, ow*

Endings: -ED and -ING

Name _____

Many new words can be formed by adding **-ed** or **-ing** to other words. When a word ends with one vowel followed by one consonant, double the consonant before adding **-ed** or **-ing.**

walk   walk**ing**
snap   snapp**ed**

Read the words and add **-ed** and **-ing** to each one. Write the new words in the blanks.

		Add **-ed**	Add **-ing**
1.	mail	*mailed*	_____
2.	hop	_____	_____
3.	plant	_____	_____
4.	talk	_____	_____
5.	chip	_____	_____

Read the list of words below. Then read each sentence that follows. Add **-ed** or **-ing** to one of the list words to complete each sentence. Write the word in the blank. The word you form must make sense in the sentence.

thank   ask   bag   stop   sweep

1. Star ___*asked*___ me to help her with some yard work.

2. We began by _____ the leaves into piles.

3. Then we _____ the leaves.

4. Star and I _____ when it became too dark to work.

5. Star's dad _____ me for my help.

Endings: -ED and -ING

Name _____

Many new words can be formed by adding **-ed** or **-ing** to other words. When a word ends in **e**, drop the **e** before adding **-ed** or **-ing**. When a word ends in a consonant followed by **y,** change **y** to **i** before adding **-ed.** Do not change **y** to **i** before adding **-ing** to a word that ends in **y.**

save	sav**ing**
hurry	hurr**ied**
carry	carry**ing**

Read the words and add **-ed** and **-ing** to each one. Write the new words in the blanks.

		Add **-ed**	Add **-ing**
1.	taste	*tasted*	_____
2.	cry	_____	_____
3.	wave	_____	_____
4.	hope	_____	_____
5.	marry	_____	_____

Read the list of words below. Then read each sentence that follows. Add **-ed** or **-ing** to one of the list words to complete each sentence. Write the word in the blank. The word you form must make sense in the sentence.

| shine | try | race | carry | skate |

1. Yoko hit the ball and ___*raced*___ toward first base.

2. My friends _____ to play softball in the rain.

3. The dog is _____ a stick in its mouth.

4. Have you ever _____ on that frozen pond?

5. I can't see because the light is _____ in my eyes.

Adding *-ed* and *-ing* to verbs in isolation and in context

Endings: -S and -ES

Name _____

Often new words can be formed by adding **-s** or **-es** to other words. To change many words, add the letter **-s.** When a word ends in a consonant followed by **y,** change the **y** to **i** and add **-es.**

laugh   laugh**s**
marry   marr**ies**

Read the words and add **-s** or **-es** to each one. Write the new words in the blanks.

1. draw   _____*draws*_____   4. sing   _____

2. copy   _____   5. walk   _____

3. study   _____   6. hurry   _____

Read the list of words below. Then read each sentence that follows. Add **-s** or **-es** to one of the list words to complete each sentence. The word you form must make sense in the sentence.

listen   need   like   try   help   study   make

1. My friend Marcos _____*likes*_____ to keep busy.

2. Before Marcos goes to school, he _____ his lunch for the next day.

3. He _____ carefully to his teacher.

4. After school he _____ young children learn to swim.

5. Marcos _____ his best to get to all of his little sister's baseball games.

6. When he gets home, Marcos does his homework and _____ for his tests.

7. I think Marcos _____ much longer days.

Endings: -ES

Name _____

Many new words can be formed by adding **-es** to other words. When a word ends in **s, ss, sh, ch,** or **x,** add **-es.**	bus bus**es** pitch pitch**es** miss miss**es** mix mix**es** fish fish**es**

Read the words. Underline the **s, ss, sh, ch,** or **x** if it comes at the end of a word. Then add **-es** to these words. Write the new words in the blanks.

1. coach   *coaches*   4. pass   _____

2. reach   _____   5. dress   _____

3. push   _____   6. wax   _____

Read the sentences and the list of words. Add **-es** to one of the list words to complete each sentence. Write the word in the blank. The word you form must make sense in the sentence.

1. After school each child ___*dresses*___ in play clothes.

2. Everyone _____ to Mrs. Bello's backyard.

3. The scout leader _____ children about camping.

4. James _____ his test when he ties the knots.

5. He _____ that he could spend the night at the lake.

6. Alma _____ the dirt from her backpack.

7. She pitches a tent while Tony _____ every step.

8. Using the campfire, Lin _____ a snack.

teach

dress

rush

watch

pass

fix

wish

brush

Adding -es to verbs in isolation and in context

Base Words and Endings

Name _____

A word to which an ending can be added is called a base word.	**reach**es

Read each word and write its base word in the blank.

1. closing   _close_

2. knowing   _____

3. skipped   _____

4. batting   _____

5. standing   _____

6. makes   _____

7. dried   _____

8. skating   _____

9. stepped   _____

10. misses   _____

11. tasted   _____

12. copies   _____

Read the list of base words below. Then read each sentence that follows. Complete the sentence by adding the ending shown beside the sentence to a word from the list. Write the new word in the blank.

bake   talk   try   run   find   fish

1. One day we were _talking_ about ways that we have fun.   -ing

2. Andrew told us he _____ in a pond near his home.   -es

3. Molly said she _____ seashells on the beach.   -s

4. Jim _____ to explain a guessing game he likes.   -ed

5. Allen said he likes _____ in a race more than anything else.   -ing

6. Jessie told how she had a lot of fun when she _____ bread for her friends.   -ed

Identifying base words; Adding endings to verbs in context

Endings: -ER and -EST

Name _____

In many words, the ending **-er** means "more." It can be used to compare two things. The ending **-est** means "most." It can be used to compare three or more things.	deep deep**er** deep deep**est**

Read the sentences and the word choices. Circle the word that makes sense in each sentence.

1. This year's dog show should be (greater, greatest) than last year's show.

2. There will be a race to see which of the many dogs can run (faster, fastest).

3. Seth hopes that his dog is (quicker, quickest) than his cousin's dog.

4. A prize will be given to the (smaller, smallest) of all the dogs.

5. The (younger, youngest) dog of all might be one of Spot's puppies.

6. My dog may be the (older, oldest) dog there, but she is also the best dog in the show!

Read each sentence and the word beside it. Add **-er** or **-est** to the word to complete the sentence. Write the new word in the blank. The word you form must make sense in the sentence.

1. I must be the _____*slowest*_____ shopper in this town.   slow

2. To save money, I try to find the _____ of all the prices.   low

3. Because I am _____ than I was last year, I must buy some new clothes.   tall

4. My dad says I might have to buy the _____ priced pants in the store.   high

5. I guess I take a _____ time choosing my things than you do.   long

Using -er or -est for comparison; Adding -er or -est to adjectives and adverbs in context

Endings: -ER and -EST

Name _____

Many new words can be formed by adding **-er** or **-est** to other words. When a word ends with one vowel followed by one consonant, double the consonant before adding **-er** or **-est**. When a word ends in **e,** drop the **e** before adding **-er** or **-est**. When a word ends in a consonant followed by **y,** change the **y** to **i** before adding **-er** or **-est**.

wet	wett**est**
wise	wis**er**
cloudy	cloud**ier**

Add **-er** and **-est** to each word below. Write the new words in the blanks.

		Add **-er**	Add **-est**
1.	busy	*busier*	_____
2.	big	_____	_____
3.	sunny	_____	_____
4.	late	_____	_____
5.	light	_____	_____

Read each sentence and the word beside it. Add **-er** or **-est** to the word to complete the sentence. Write the new word in the blank. The word you form must make sense in the sentence.

1. Lance's shop has the ____*cutest*____ stuffed toys I've seen. cute

2. The orange cat is _____ than my yellow cat. fat

3. That clown has the _____ hat that I've seen. funny

4. You'd like seeing the deer that is _____ than a person. tall

5. The shop has the _____ toys of any store in town. fine

Endings: -ER and -EST

Name _____

Read each sentence and the word shown below the blank. Add **-er** or **-est** to the word to complete the sentence. Write the new word in the blank.

1. This book is ___*sillier*___ than the book about the pink turtle.
   (silly)

2. Will the stove get _____ than it is now?
   (hot)

3. Can you make this room look _____ than it looked before?
   (neat)

4. Please buy the _____ poster you can find.
   (bright)

5. Is that the _____ of all the hot-air balloons in the show?
   (big)

6. Where can I buy the _____ flowers in town?
   (nice)

7. The day of the school play is our _____ day of the year.
   (busy)

8. This metal ring is _____ than the wooden ring I used to have.
   (loose)

9. Ellen's apartment is _____ to the school than mine is.
   (close)

10. The baby looked _____ after she took her nap.
    (happy)

11. Brenda's dog is _____ than Ken's dog.
    (fat)

Adding *-er* or *-est* to adjectives in context

Endings

Name _____

Read the list of words below. Then read each sentence that follows. Complete the sentence by adding one of the endings shown beside the sentence to a word from the list. Write the new word in the blank. The word you form must make sense in the sentence.

fish	bat	chase	study	jump	bake

1. Tim's father ____*bakes*____ bread in the new oven.   -s, -es

2. Peggy _____ for trout in a stream near the park.   -s, -es

3. Will you be _____ in the next baseball game?   -ed, -ing

4. Len _____ his spelling words each morning.   -es, -ing

5. Elena _____ into the swimming pool from the diving board. -ed, -ing

6. Today I _____ my kitten around the house.   -ed, -ing

Add **-er** and **-est** to each word below. Write the new words in the blanks.

	Add **-er**	Add **-est**
1. slow	*slower*	_____
2. sad	_____	_____
3. fine	_____	_____
4. pretty	_____	_____
5. large	_____	_____
6. loud	_____	_____

Review of adding *-ed*, *-ing*, *-s*, or *-es* to verbs in context; Adding *-er* and *-est* to adjectives

Plurals: -S and -ES

Name _____

A word that stands for one of something is a singular word. A word that stands for two or more of something is a plural word. To write the plural form of most words, add **-s.** To form the plural of a word that ends in **s, ss, sh, ch,** or **x,** add **-es.** To form the plural of a word that ends in a consonant followed by **y,** change the **y** to **i** and add **-es.**

toy	toy**s**
lunch	lunch**es**
baby	bab**ies**

Read the words. Write the plural form of each one.

1. shoe _____*shoes*_____

2. watch _____

3. brush _____

4. party _____

5. boss _____

6. room _____

7. puppy _____

8. fox _____

Read the sentences and the list of words. Write the plural form of a word from the list to complete each sentence. The word you form must make sense in the sentence.

1. We can ride our _____*bikes*_____ to the market.

2. Let's go after we eat and do the _____.

3. Eva wants us to buy some _____ that can be planted.

4. She will plant them in the ground in straight _____.

5. We can pay for the flowers with five dollars and some

   _____.

6. We will ask for _____ to hold the daisies we buy.

row

box

dish

six

bike

penny

daisy

story

Forming plurals in isolation and in context: -s and es

Plurals: Changing *F* to *V*

Name _____

To write the plural form of most words that end in **f** or **fe**, change the **f** or **fe** to **v** and add **-es**.	leaf	lea**ves**
	life	li**ves**

Read each sentence and the words beside it. Write the plural form of one of the words to complete each sentence. The word you form must make sense in the sentence.

1. The cook uses sharp *knives* to cut the meat.　　　　life
knife

2. How many _____ of bread are needed to make forty sandwiches?　　　　loaf
leaf

3. In this make-believe story, a group of _____ makes a family very happy.　　　　shelf
elf

4. Most of those _____ were born last week.　　　　calf
half

5. The tree grows new _____ each spring.　　　　leaf
life

6. This book tells about the _____ of well-known men and women.　　　　life
loaf

7. In the play, a bank was robbed by two _____.　　　　thief
knife

8. My brother and sister learned how to build _____ for their books.　　　　shelf
self

Irregular Plurals

Name _____

The plurals of some words are formed by changing the spelling of their singular forms.

child - children	man - men	woman - women
tooth - teeth	foot - feet	mouse - mice
goose - geese		

The plural forms of some words can be the same as their singular forms.

sheep   deer   fish

Read each set of sentences and its list of words. Write the plural form of a word from the list to complete each sentence. The word you form must make sense in the sentence.

1. _Children_ will enjoy seeing the puppet show.

2. How much wool can you get from six _____?

3. I have seen _____ flying over our campsite.

4. Many women and _____ will vote tomorrow.

5. I found a nest of baby _____ that were each smaller than my thumb.

man
fish
Child
foot
goose
sheep
mouse

---

1. Every morning, Dad asks me if I have brushed my
   _____.

2. We need more men and _____ to drive the school buses.

3. If we wait near the woods, we might see some _____.

4. The new shoes I am wearing make my _____ hurt.

5. Joy came home carrying a pail filled with _____ that she caught at the lake.

fish
woman
deer
tooth
child
foot
mouse

Forming irregular plurals in context

Plurals

Name _____

Read the paragraphs and the list of words. Write the plural form of a word from the list to complete each sentence. The words you form must make sense in the paragraph.

I think you will like this store better than the *stores*

we shopped in before. It is full of things for _____ under

the age of twelve. The clothing part of the store has jeans, shirts, and

_____. Another part of the store has _____   watch

to tell time, as well as rings and bracelets.   baby

calf

Most children like to look at the toys. They are in the biggest part of   store

the store. The _____ are full of every kind of toy. There   peach

are dolls that look like newborn _____, and dolls that are   shelf

dressed like grown men and _____. I have seen sets of   dress

_____ you could eat from and small sinks and stoves.   dish

There are also toy foods, such as apples and _____.   penny

child

You might like seeing the stuffed animals like those puppies and   game

_____. I never leave the store without looking at the   woman

_____ that can be played by one or more players. You

can see why I save my _____ before I visit this store!

Showing Ownership

Name _____

| To make most words show ownership, add an apostrophe (') and **s.** In the example, **dog's bone,** the **'s** shows that the bone belongs to the dog. | dog**'s** bone |

Rewrite each group of words below, adding **'s** to form words that show ownership.

1. the horse that Bruce owns   *Bruce's horse*

2. the sock that the baby wears   _____

3. the windows of a truck   _____

4. the backpack that Sal owns   _____

5. the game that belongs to Kim   _____

6. the paw of a cat   _____

Read each sentence and the words beside it. Add **'s** to one of the words to complete the sentence. The word you form must make sense in the sentence.

1. The _*bank's*_ doors open each day at nine o'clock.

bank
book

2. My _____ office is in the center of the town.

apple
aunt

3. Her _____ speech was heard by many people.

father
farm

4. The _____ flowers are light pink.

brush
bush

5. My math _____ writing is easy to read.

teacher
tractor

112

Showing Ownership

Name _____

To make a singular word show ownership, add an apostrophe (') and **s**. To make a plural word that ends in **s** show ownership, add just an apostrophe. In the examples, **'s** shows that the bones belong to one dog, and **s'** shows that the bones belong to more than one dog.

dog**'s** bones
dog**s'** bones

Read the words and look at the pictures. Circle the words that tell about each picture.

girl's gloves (girls' gloves)	tree's bark trees' bark	truck's wheels trucks' wheels
dog's food dogs' food	boy's photos boys' photos	skunk's stripes skunks' stripes

Rewrite each group of words below, adding **'** or **'s** to the underlined word to show ownership.

1. the wings of the <u>birds</u>   *birds' wings*

2. the tent that is used by the <u>scouts</u> _____

3. the house that belongs to a <u>teacher</u> _____

4. the office used by two <u>dentists</u> _____

5. the covers of the <u>books</u> _____

6. the tail of a <u>monkey</u> _____

Showing Ownership

Name _____

Read each sentence and the words shown below the blank. Write the word that makes sense in the sentence.

1. The _____*dog's*_____ tail is short and brown.
   (dog's, dogs')

2. The two _____ steering wheels are the same color.
   (truck's, trucks')

3. That _____ stripes are green and white.
   (flag's, flags')

4. The _____ birthdays are on the same day.
   (boy's, boys')

5. Did you see _____ new puppy?
   (Marys', Mary's)

6. I could see the _____ heads through the little window.
   (cat's, cats')

7. My youngest _____ blocks are on her bedroom floor.
   (sister's, sisters')

8. We found _____ hammer under the steps.
   (Mother's, Mothers')

9. The _____ coat is always kept clean.
   (kittens', kitten's)

10. The _____ floors are made of wood.
    (room's, rooms')

11. My _____ nose was sunburned yesterday.
    (friend's, friends')

12. The _____ engines were made in this city.
    (car's, cars')

Using singular and plural possessives in context

Plurals and Showing Ownership

Name _____

Read the words and write the plural form of each one.

1. bicycle   *bicycles*

2. wolf   _____

3. school   _____

4. baby   _____

5. child   _____

6. box   _____

7. apple   _____

8. party   _____

9. glass   _____

10. man   _____

11. patch   _____

12. deer   _____

13. elf   _____

14. puppy   _____

Rewrite each group of words below, adding ' or 's to the underlined word to show ownership.

1. the whiskers of the <u>cats</u>   *cats' whiskers*

2. the field that is used by the <u>players</u>   _____

3. the apartment that belongs to <u>Joan</u>   _____

4. the library used by the <u>teachers</u>   _____

5. the playground owned by the <u>school</u>   _____

6. the hats worn by the <u>fire fighters</u>   _____

7. the smile of the <u>child</u>   _____

8. the backpack that belongs to <u>Bob</u>   _____

Endings and Plurals

Name _____

Read each sentence and the word beside it. Complete each sentence by adding one of the endings shown below to the word. Write the new word in the blank. The word you form must make sense in the sentence.

-ed   -ing   -s   -es   -er   -est

1. A storm began while we were _*playing*_ in the yard.   play

2. That is the _____ hat I have ever seen!   silly

3. A few of us _____ the logs for the fire.   carry

4. Aunt Janet _____ me every time I visit.   thank

5. When Dave's football clothes are dirty, he _____ them.   wash

6. The crowd _____ when the show was over.   clap

7. Celina seems _____ today than she was yesterday.   happy

8. Every afternoon a jet _____ over our house.   fly

Read the words and write the plural form of each one.

1. brush   _*brushes*_   7. mouse   _____

2. friend   _____   8. city   _____

3. box   _____   9. match   _____

4. book   _____   10. shelf   _____

5. buggy   _____   11. sheep   _____

6. knife   _____   12. class   _____

Assessment of adding endings to base words in context; Forming plurals

Showing Ownership

<u>Name</u> _____

Read each sentence and the words beside it. Write the word that makes sense in each sentence.

1. This spelling _____*book's*_____ pages are ripped.

book's
books'

2. Her _____ bedrooms are painted red and blue.

brother's
brothers'

3. Our many _____ leaves are different shades of green.

tree's
trees'

4. _____ school was built last year.

Jack's
Jacks'

5. The three _____ noses were shiny and red.

clown's
clowns'

6. The bedroom _____ ring woke me up.

phone's
phones'

7. The _____ lawn is always green.

park's
parks'

8. All of these _____ frames are made of wood and metal.

picture's
pictures'

9. The _____ trunks are strong enough to carry logs.

elephant's
elephants'

10. My oldest _____ shoe size is a five.

sister's
sisters'

Reading and Writing Wrap-Up

Name _____

The Boy Who Cried "Wolf!"

This is a story that teaches something important about life. Read to see if you can find out what it is.

Once there was a boy who looked after sheep. He had nothing to do all day but watch the sheep, and he was bored.

One day the boy thought of a way to have some fun, so he ran into the village shouting, "Wolf! Wolf! A wolf is after the sheep!"

All the people in the village left their work to help the boy. But when they reached the place where the sheep were grazing, there was no wolf in sight. The boy laughed at the people for believing his trick. The next day the boy played the same trick. Now he was having fun.

On the third day, the boy saw a hungry wolf coming near the flock, and he got very frightened. He ran as fast as his legs would carry him to the village. "Help!" he cried. "A wolf is going to kill the sheep!"

But this time the people did not leave their work to help the boy. They said, "That boy is just trying to fool us again by telling another lie." When the boy returned to the sheep, he saw that the wolf had killed them all.

The people were very angry when they found out the boy had not been telling a lie this time. They said, "People who tell lies cannot be believed even when they say something that is true."

A. Answer the following questions.

1. What was the job of the boy in the story?

   _____

2. Why did the boy play a trick?

   _____

3. What did the people do the first time the boy played his trick?

   _____

Application of reading and comprehension skills in a literature context

Name _____

B. Check the two words in each line that have the same meaning in the story.

1. _____ play   _____ fool   _____ trick

2. _____ flock   _____ sheep   _____ grazing

C. Answer the following questions.
   1. What does this story teach about life?

   _____

   _____

   2. Do you think the people were right or wrong not to believe the boy the third time he cried, "Wolf"? Tell why or why not.

   _____

   _____

D. Write a story about one of the following sayings.

   If you want something to be done right, do it yourself.
   In time of trouble, you find out who your true friends are.
   Those who harm others often end up harming themselves.

   _____

   _____

   _____

   _____

   _____

   _____

Application of thinking and writing skills in a literature context

Compound Words

Name _____

| A compound word is formed by joining two smaller words together. | dog + house = doghouse |

Read each compound word and write the two words that form it.

1. waterfall _____*water*_____ _____*fall*_____

2. snowflakes _____ _____

3. grandson _____ _____

4. bookcase _____ _____

5. doorbell _____ _____

6. rainstorm _____ _____

7. lighthouse _____ _____

Read the sentences. Circle the two compound words in each sentence.

1. Can you use your (snowplow) on our (driveway)?

2. I found a starfish and a few seashells on the beach.

3. Jean will fold the bedspread that goes in her bedroom.

4. My grandfather makes homemade bean soup.

5. I must have left my raincoat on the playground.

6. Have you ever watched a sunset from the tall building downtown?

7. The plants will not grow without sunshine.

Identifying words that form compound words; Identifying compound words in context

Compound Words

Name _____

Read the words in each list below. Draw lines to match the words that form compound words.

book	place	side	noon
rain	fall	snow	paper
pan	day	after	walk
fire	case	fire	storm
birth	cakes	news	wood

Read the list of words below. Then read the sentences that follow. Write the word from the list that makes sense in each sentence.

notebook   cookbook   sometimes   something   oatmeal
airplane   rowboat   grandmother   airport

1. I plan to write to my *grandmother*, who lives in New York.

2. She will enjoy reading about my _____ ride on the lake.

3. She may remember the time we went to the city _____.

4. We flew in an _____ that took us over the town.

5. We did that because Grandmother wanted me to try

_____ new.

6. She _____ wants me to taste something I've never
eaten before.

7. Once she tried to make me eat _____.

8. As a joke, I bought her a new _____ to read.

9. I could fill a _____ with stories about Grandmother and me!

Compound Words

Name _____

Read the sentences below. Use two words from each sentence to form a compound word. Write the compound word in the blank.

1.   A bird that is blue is called a ___*bluebird*___.

2.   A walk near the side of a road is a _____.

3.   A cloth that covers a table is a _____.

4.   The bud of a rose is a _____.

5.   A ball that is thrown through a basket is a _____.

6.   A brush that is used to clean each tooth is a _____.

7.   Work that is done for school is called _____.

8.   A shell that can be found near the sea is a _____.

9.   Corn that you can pop is called _____.

10. A bell that is near the door of a house is a _____.

11. A pot that holds tea is a _____.

12. Wood that is used to build a fire is called _____.

13. The print of a foot made in sand is called a _____.

14. Work done at home is _____.

15. A tub for a bath is a _____.

16. A boat that has a sail is a _____.

Forming compound words in context

Contractions

Name _____

A contraction is a short way to write two words. It is written by putting two words together and leaving out a letter or letters. An apostrophe (') takes the place of the letters that are left out. The word **won't** is a special contraction made from the words **will** and **not.**

is + not = **isn't**
will + not = **won't**
we + are = **we're**
I + will = **I'll**

Read the list of contractions below. Then read the pairs of words that follow. Write a contraction from the list that stands for each word pair.

| it's | she'll | weren't |
| we'd | hadn't | they're |

1. had not   _*hadn't*_   4. she will   _____

2. were not   _____   5. we would   _____

3. they are   _____   6. it is   _____

Read each sentence and the pair of words shown below the blank. Complete the sentence by writing the contraction that stands for the word pair.

1. Does he know that ____*we're*____ coming home early?
   (we are)

2. Tammy _____ find the letter she wrote.
   (could not)

3. John _____ ready to swim in the deep end of the pool.
   (was not)

4. We _____ go to school in the summer.
   (do not)

5. Did you know that _____ been visiting their friends?
   (they have)

6. Ellen _____ be able to come to our party.
   (will not)

Contractions

Name _____

Read the contractions below. Then write the two words for which each contraction stands.

1. wouldn't   *would not*   6. he'll   _____

2. we've   _____   7. hasn't   _____

3. didn't   _____   8. she's   _____

4. that's   _____   9. won't   _____

5. we'd   _____   10. I've   _____

Read each sentence and the contraction shown below the blank. Complete the sentence by writing the two words for which the contraction stands.

1. ___*I would*___ like to move to a warmer part of the country.
    (I'd)

2. It _____ snow where you live, does it?
       (doesn't)

3. _____ not seen a snowflake since you moved there.
       (You've)

4. I _____ be able to go sled riding if I lived where you live.
       (wouldn't)

5. _____ not cold enough to go ice skating, either.
       (It's)

6. _____ not sure I want to move after all.
       (I'm)

Identifying words that form contractions in isolation and in context

Contractions

Name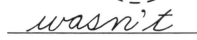

Read each sentence and find the two words in it that can be made into a contraction. Circle the two words and write the contraction in the blank.

1. The city zoo (was not) far from our school building.

   wasn't

2. It did not take the bus driver long to get there.

   _____

3. Kelly and Ross could not wait to see the animals.

   _____

4. They had been counting the days until the trip.

   _____

5. Kelly says that she is going to work in a zoo someday.

   _____

Read the sentences and the list of contractions. Write the contraction that makes sense in each sentence. The word you write must make sense in the sentence.

1. _Shouldn't_ Amy read the story to the class?

2. Jordan and Juan _____ here when she read it before.

3. I think _____ be sorry they missed the funny ending.

4. I told Ms. Mendes that we _____ made the story into a play.

5. She told us _____ what had been planned.

6. We can start planning after _____ heard the story.

they'll

that's

won't

didn't

Shouldn't

we've

weren't

should've

Compound Words and Contractions

Name _____

Read the clues below. Use two words from each clue to form a compound word.
Write the compound word in the blank.

1. a coat worn in the rain   *raincoat*

2. a boat that you can row   _____

3. a tie that is worn around the neck   _____

4. work done around the house   _____

5. a book that tells you how to cook   _____

6. water from a stream that falls over a high place _____

7. a bell that is rung at the door of a home   _____

Read the word pairs below. Then write the contraction that stands for each
word pair.

1. we are   *we're*   8. have not   _____

2. will not   _____   9. they have   _____

3. he will   _____   10. can not   _____

4. you would   _____   11. I am   _____

5. are not   _____   12. she had   _____

6. they are   _____   13. do not   _____

7. we have   _____   14. there is   _____

Review of forming compound words; Forming contractions

Compound Words and Contractions

Name _____

Read the list of words below. Then read the sentences that follow. Choose a word from the list to complete the compound word in each sentence. The compound word you form must make sense in the sentence.

place	port	work
case	way	room

1. I read my book and finished my home _work_.

2. Each of my books is now in the book_____.

3. I took my bath and cleaned the tub in the bath_____.

4. I helped my mom build a fire in the fire_____.

5. Soon, Dad will bring my uncle home from the air_____.

6. I can't wait until I see them pull into the drive_____.

Read each sentence and the pair of words beside it. Complete each sentence with a contraction that stands for the word pair.

1. _I'll_____ show you how to make paper airplanes.   I will

2. _____ not as hard to make as you may think.   They are

3. _____ the pattern for the plane you want to make?   Where is

4. I think _____ enjoy using this colored paper.   you would

5. We _____ tried folding the heavier white paper.   have not

6. _____ we start with the smallest plane?   Should not

Prefixes: *UN-* and *DIS-*

Name _____

| A prefix is a letter or group of letters that can be added to the beginning of a word. The prefixes **un-** and **dis-** mean "not" or "the opposite of." For example, the word **unlock** means "the opposite of lock." The word **dislike** means "not like." | **un** + lock = **un**lock
dis + like = **dis**like |

Read the list of words below. Then read each sentence that follows. Add **un-** to one of the list words to complete each sentence. Write the new word in the blank. The word you form must make sense in the sentence.

safe   load   happy   lock

1. We need help to *unload* the logs from the truck.

2. The busy street is _____ for the children who walk to school.

3. The small child looked _____ when she let go of her balloon.

4. You will need a key to _____ the front door.

Read the list of words below. Then read each sentence that follows. Add **dis-** to one of the list words to complete each sentence. Write the new word in the blank. The word you form must make sense in the sentence.

cover   connect   agree   liked   color

1. The bright light of the sun may _____*discolor*_____ the camper's tent.

2. The scientists hope to _____ a cure for the illness.

3. Joey _____ singing in the class play.

4. Ms. Miller will _____ the wire before she fixes the lamp.

5. Because we _____, we should talk about the problem.

Forming words with prefixes *un-* and *dis-*; Words containing prefixes in context

Prefixes: *RE-* and *PRE-*

Name _____

The prefix **re-** means "again." For example, the word **refill** means "fill again." The prefix **pre-** means "before." The word **prepay** means "pay before."

re + fill = **re**fill
pre + pay = **pre**pay

Read the clues. Add **re-** or **pre-** to the underlined base word to form a word that matches the clue.

1. to <u>wrap</u> again *rewrap*

2. to <u>test</u> before _____

3. to <u>write</u> again _____

4. to <u>paint</u> again _____

5. to <u>use</u> again _____

6. before a <u>game</u> _____

Read each sentence and the words beside it. Write the word that makes sense in each sentence.

1. Ardis brought a book home from her *preschool* class.

retell
preschool
pregame

2. Do you know how to _____ the part on the bike?

reread
replay
replace

3. The bill was _____ a week ago.

prepaid
pregame
replayed

4. We watched the band march in the _____ show.

retell
prepaid
pregame

5. Are you able to _____ the tale you heard last night?

reread
retell
preheat

6. Please _____ the story for the class.

replace
replay
reread

Prefixes: OVER- and MIS-

Name _____

The prefix **over-** means "too much." For example, the word **overdo** means "to do too much." The prefix **mis-** means "badly" or "wrongly." For example, the word **misuse** means "to use wrongly."

over + do = **over**do
mis + use = **mis**use

Read the list of words below. Then read each sentence that follows. Add **over-** to one of the list words to complete each sentence. Write the new word in the blank. The word you form must make sense in the sentence.

eat   sleep   cook   load   flow

1. Did you _____*oversleep*_____ on the first day of school?

2. Be careful not to _____ your book bag.

3. The rain made the river _____.

4. The good food made me want to _____.

5. If you _____ the meat, it will be dry.

Read the list of words below. Then read each sentence that follows. Add **mis-** to one of the list words to complete each sentence. Write the new word in the blank. The word you form must make sense in the sentence.

understand   spell   place   treat   lead

1. If you _____*mistreat*_____ your bike, it will not run well.

2. When you _____ a word, cross it out and write it correctly.

3. Did you _____ what needed to be done?

4. If you _____ your homework, you must find it or redo it.

5. That sign will _____ travelers.

Forming words with prefixes *over-* and *mis-*; Words containing prefixes in context

Prefixes

Name _____

Read each sentence and the word beside it. Add **un-, pre-,** or **over-** to the word to complete each sentence. Write the new word in the blank. The word you form must make sense in the sentence.

1. The ___*unfair*___ rules were changed.   fair

2. I _____ the cost at the time I ordered.   paid

3. If you don't wake her, she will _____.   sleep

4. My dog _____ when there is too much food in the dish.   eats

5. Because I lost the game, I felt _____.   lucky

6. Scott talks about his _____ class.   school

Read each sentence and the word beside it. Add **dis-, re-,** or **mis-** to the word to complete each sentence. Write the new word in the blank. The word you form must make sense in the sentence.

1. If you ___*disagree*___ with me, let me know.   agree

2. Grandma will _____ many of her stories.   tell

3. I often _____ the time when I get busy.   judge

4. I will _____ the chicken soup for lunch.   heat

5. We saw the rabbit _____ from sight into the red hat.   appear

6. If you _____ the sign, you will get lost.   read

Suffixes: -FUL and -LESS

Name _____

A suffix is a letter or group of letters that can be added to the end of a word. The suffix **-ful** usually means "full of." For example, the word **helpful** means "full of help." The suffix **-less** usually means "without." The word **hopeless** means "without hope."

help + **ful** = help**ful**
hope + **less** = hope**less**

Read the words below. Form new words by adding the suffix **-ful** or **-less** to the words. Write each word under the correct heading.

end   hand   wonder   friend   play   cloud   forget   home

Add **-ful**	Add **-less**
handful	

Read the sentences and the list of words. Write the word from the list that makes sense in each sentence.

1. I was _____*careless*_____ when I lost my math paper.

2. Put a small _____ of salt into the soup.

3. I slept well and had a _____ night.

4. We are _____ that we have friends like you.

5. I am glad the snake we saw is _____.

6. The list of jobs to do at home seems _____.

careless
restful
helpful
harmless
sleepless
thankful
spoonful
endless

Forming words with suffixes -ful and -less; Words containing suffixes in context

Suffixes: -Y and -LY

Name _____

The suffixes **-y** and **-ly** can be added to some words. For example, a day with **rain** is a **rainy** day. Something done in a **nice** way is done **nicely.**

rain + **y** = rain**y**
nice + **ly** = nice**ly**

Read the list of words below. Then read each sentence that follows. Add **-y** to one of the list words to complete each sentence. Write the new word in the blank. The word you form must make sense in the sentence.

| frost | cloud | stick | luck | squeak |

1. We were _____*lucky*_____ to get five tickets for the early show last Saturday.

2. I spilled some glue, and my desk is now _____.

3. We didn't see much sunshine because the sky was _____.

4. My new boots make a _____ sound when I walk.

5. Because it is cold outdoors, our windows look white and _____.

Read the list of words below. Then read each sentence that follows. Add **-ly** to one of the list words to complete each sentence. Write the new word in the blank. The word you form must make sense in the sentence.

| soft | week | quick | friend | slow |

1. Because he walked _____*slowly*_____, he missed the bus.

2. If we get dressed _____, we can go sled riding before we eat.

3. My older brother reads a _____ newspaper.

4. She played the song so _____ that we could hardly hear it.

5. We had fun at the party because we met some _____ people.

Suffixes: -ABLE and -ISH

Name _____

The suffix **-able** means "can be" or "able to be." For example, the word **washable** means "can be washed." The suffix **-ish** means "like" or "somewhat." The word **childish** means "like a child."

wash + **able** = wash**able**
child + **ish** = child**ish**

Read the words below. Form new words by adding the suffix **-able** or **-ish** to the words. Write each word under the correct heading.

yellow   baby   break   pass   girl   like   clown   change

Add **-able**	Add **-ish**
breakable	_____
_____	_____
_____	_____
_____	_____

Read the sentences and the list of words. Add **-able** or **-ish** to one of the list words to complete each sentence. Write the word in the blank. The word you form must make sense in the sentence.

1. The low shelf makes the toys _*reachable*_.

2. The pond's water looks _____.

3. It is _____ to cross the street without looking both ways.

4. That page got wet, so the words are no longer _____.

5. You can get the stain out of a _____ shirt.

wash

green

reach

fool

read

Forming words with suffixes *-able* and *-ish*: Words containing suffixes in context

Suffixes

Name _____

Read each sentence and the suffixes beside it. Add one of the suffixes to the word shown below the blank to complete the sentence. The word you form must make sense in the sentence.

1. Please speak ___*loudly*___ when you give your speech.
    (loud)

    -ful
    -ly

2. Berta has brown eyes and long, _____ brown hair.
    (curl)

    -y
    -ful

3. After looking for my bike for an hour, I felt _____.
    (hope)

    -less
    -ly

4. Pedro's _____ act was really funny.
    (clown)

    -ly
    -ish

5. The sun was shining, and the sky was _____.
    (cloud)

    -less
    -ful

6. I can help you put some oil on this _____ door.
    (squeak)

    -y
    -ly

7. The children watching the puppet show looked _____.
    (cheer)

    -ish
    -ful

8. Billy is _____ to all of his team members.
    (friend)

    -ly
    -able

9. I will be _____ and tell you how I feel.
    (truth)

    -ful
    -less

10. Marta's new sweater is _____.
    (wash)

    -less
    -able

Prefixes and Suffixes

Name _____

Read the clues. Add one of the prefixes or suffixes from the list to each underlined base word to form a word that matches the clue.

1. full of <u>truth</u>   *truthful* _____

2. having <u>frost</u>   _____

3. the opposite of <u>agree</u>   _____

4. to <u>write</u> again   _____

5. the opposite of <u>trust</u>   _____

6. to <u>pay</u> before   _____

7. without <u>pain</u>   _____

8. full of <u>care</u>   _____

pre-

dis-

re-

-ful

-less

-y

---

1. to <u>do</u> too much   _____

2. not <u>true</u>   _____

3. like a <u>child</u>   _____

4. <u>read</u> wrongly   _____

5. every <u>week</u>   _____

6. able to <u>change</u>   _____

7. to <u>sleep</u> too much   _____

8. not <u>hurt</u>   _____

un-

over-

mis-

-ly

-able

-ish

Review of forming words with prefixes and suffixes

Prefixes and Suffixes

Name _____

Read the list of words below. Circle the prefix or suffix in each word.

thought(ful)	thankless	readable	mistreat
greenish	disconnect	fairly	unsafe
overflow	replace	preheat	rusty

Read the list of words below. Then read the sentences that follow. Write the word from the list that makes sense in each sentence.

unpack	helpless	disappear	rewrap	restful	misplace
rocky	overload	pregame	neatly	grayish	breakable

1. The book about magic tricks shows you how to make a ball *disappear*.

2. There will be a _____ show on the football field.

3. When Bill gets home, he will _____ his suitcases.

4. Please _____ the leftover food and put it in the freezer.

5. We felt _____ when we couldn't fix the car.

6. Climbing up the _____ hillside took us most of the day.

7. Did you _____ the books you brought home?

8. I will be careful when I wash the _____ vase.

9. My new cat has a _____ coat and white paws.

10. Because I felt ill, I was told to have a _____ day at home.

11. The books and papers are stacked _____ on the shelves.

12. The truck will not run well if you _____ it.

Syllables

Name <u>   </u>

Many words are made of small parts called syllables. Because each syllable has one vowel sound, a word has as many syllables as it has vowel sounds. The word **stone** has one vowel sound, so it has one syllable. The word **raincoat** has two vowel sounds, so it has two syllables.

Name the pictures. Write the number of syllables you hear in each picture name.

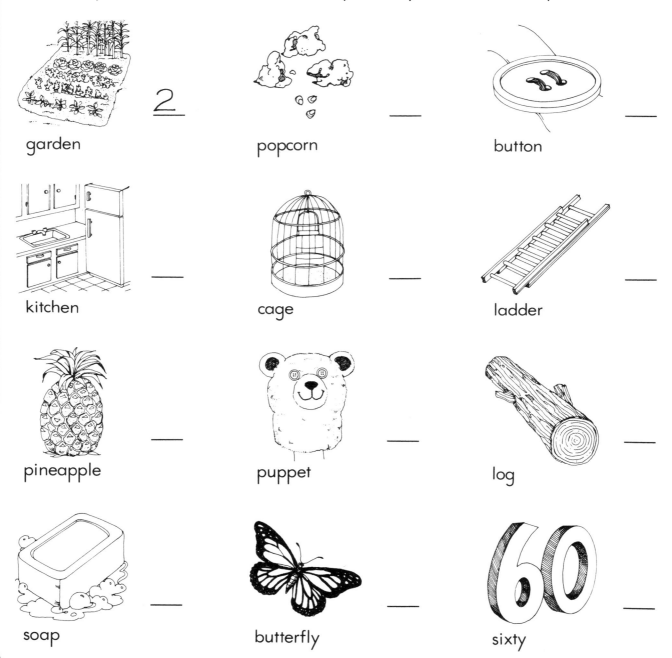

garden   _2_

popcorn   ___

button   ___

kitchen   ___

cage   ___

ladder   ___

pineapple   ___

puppet   ___

log   ___

soap   ___

butterfly   ___

sixty   ___

Identifying the number of syllables in a word

Syllables

A compound word should be divided into syllables between the words that make it compound.

rain/bow

Read the words below. Circle each compound word. Then write each compound word and draw a line between its syllables.

1. (sunset) _____*sun/set*_____

2. summer _____

3. someone _____

4. lighthouse _____

5. trouble _____

6. notebook _____

7. highway _____

8. jumping _____

9. broom _____

10. railroad _____

11. starfish _____

12. spray _____

13. doghouse _____

14. baseball _____

15. homemade _____

16. puppy _____

17. without _____

18. bedroom _____

19. teapot _____

20. birthday _____

21. toothbrush _____

22. raindrop _____

23. lifeboat _____

24. sidewalk _____

25. snowflake _____

26. throat _____

27. downtown _____

28. father _____

Syllables

Name _____

A word that has a prefix or suffix can be divided into syllables between the prefix or suffix and the base word.

un/tie
dark/ness

Read the list of words and the sentences. Divide each list word into syllables by drawing a line between the syllables. Then write the word from the list that makes sense in each sentence.

un/tie
pretest
sleepless
thoughtful
refill
dislike
neatly
softly
rewrite
rainy

1. Today I will ____*rewrite*____ my story with a pen.

2. We will _____ the car's gas tank before we start on our trip.

3. Please help me _____ this string so I can open the box.

4. I will sing the song _____ to the baby.

5. Before he started the lesson, the teacher gave us a

   _____ to see what we knew.

6. Calling me on my birthday was a _____ thing for you to do.

7. Because the dog barked for many hours, I had a

   _____ night.

8. I _____ walking to school on rainy days.

9. It is hard to ride a bike on a _____ day.

10. All of the books were _____ placed on the shelves.

Dividing words containing affixes into syllables; Using two-syllable words in context

Syllables

Name _____

When a word has two consonants between two vowels, the word is usually divided between the two consonants.	mon/key cir/cus
	VC/CV VC/CV

Read the list of words. Write each word and draw a line between its syllables.

1. magnet   *mag/net*

2. blanket   _____

3. harvest   _____

4. lumber   _____

5. butter   _____

6. corner   _____

7. mistake   _____

8. happen   _____

9. basket   _____

10. dentist _____

Read each sentence and the words below each blank. Complete each sentence by writing the word that has the VC/CV pattern. Draw a line between its syllables.

1. Last ___*win/ter*___ we went to see Grandmother and Grandfather.
   (weekend, winter)

2. We can buy food for the picnic at the _____.
   (market, store)

3. Did you leave a _____ on my desk this morning?
   (paper, pencil)

4. The _____ sometimes wears a fancy crown.
   (lady, princess)

5. Place a _____ next to each plate on the table.
   (napkin, fork)

6. The baby held a _____ spoon in her hand.
   (tiny, silver)

Syllables

Name _____

Words that have one consonant between two vowels can be divided into syllables in two ways. When you see a word that has one consonant between two vowels, say the word. If the first vowel sound is long, divide the word after the first vowel. If the first vowel sound is short, divide the word after the consonant that follows the vowel.

1 ē/ven   pā/per
   V/CV   V/C V

2 vĭs/it   mĕt/al
   VC/V   VC/V

Read the list of words. Write each word. Mark the first vowel of the word with ˘ if it stands for the short sound or ˉ if it stands for the long sound. Then draw a line between its syllables.

1. label *lā/bel*

2. moment _____

3. cabin _____

4. lemon _____

5. travel _____

6. music _____

7. open _____

8. salad _____

9. robin _____

10. silent _____

11. pupil _____

12. petal _____

13. fever _____

14. planet _____

15. finish _____

16. famous _____

17. siren _____

18. pedal _____

19. tiger _____

20. wagon _____

Dividing words with the V/CV and VC/V patterns into syllables

Syllables

Name _____

Read the list of words. Write each word and draw a line between its syllables. Mark the first vowel of the word with ˘ if it stands for the short sound or ¯ if it stands for the long sound.

1. camel   *căm/el*

2. acorn   _____

3. palace   _____

4. damage   _____

5. paper   _____

6. closet   _____

7. famous   _____

8. medal   _____

9. bacon   _____

10. minus   _____

Read the list of words and the sentences. Divide each list word into syllables by drawing a line between the syllables. Then write the word from the list that makes sense in each sentence.

h u/m a n

s e c o n d

s h a d o w

f l a v o r

h a b i t

p o n y

p i l o t

s h i v e r

m e t a l

h o t e l

1. I learned how to ride a ___*pony*___ when I was young.

2. Greg won _____ prize in the art contest.

3. Our room in the _____ is big enough for the whole family.

4. The _____ can fly the airplane at night.

5. Choose the _____ of ice cream you like best.

6. The shed is made of wood and _____.

7. Packing an apple in my lunch is a _____ for me.

8. Each February we wait to see if the groundhog will see its

_____.

Syllables

Name _____

Read the words below. Write each word and draw a line between its syllables.

1. chapter *chap/ter*

2. undress _____

3. cozy _____

4. squeaky _____

5. magic _____

6. hopeless _____

7. firewood _____

8. model _____

9. picnic _____

10. truthful _____

11. button _____

12. oatmeal _____

13. closet _____

14. pretest _____

15. never _____

16. minus _____

17. doorbell _____

18. notice _____

19. painless _____

20. distrust _____

21. lemon _____

22. sunny _____

23. highway _____

24. later _____

25. harbor _____

26. wishbone _____

27. reuse _____

28. salad _____

29. acorn _____

30. slowly _____

31. unsafe _____

32. rewrite _____

Review of dividing words into syllables

Syllables

Name _____

Read the words below. Write each word and draw a line between its syllables.

1. refill   _____re/fill_____

2. friendly   _____

3. yellow   _____

4. human   _____

5. untie   _____

6. displease   _____

7. pencil   _____

8. notebook   _____

9. petal   _____

10. cheerful   _____

Read the list of words and the sentences. Divide each list word into syllables by drawing a line between the syllables. Then write the word from the list that makes sense in each sentence.

t r a v/e l
c l o u d y
s t a r f i s h
b e d r o o m
f a m o u s
n e a t l y
m i s t a k e
u n l o a d
d o c t o r
f i n i s h

1. I visit the _____doctor_____ at least once a year.

2. The team will _____ to the city next weekend.

3. A _____ singer will sing in this show.

4. I made only one _____ on my math test.

5. The _____ sky made us afraid that we wouldn't be able to have our picnic.

6. When I _____ my homework, I can watch the television show.

7. There are two beds in my _____.

8. Please help us _____ the boxes from the truck.

Reading and Writing Wrap-Up

Name _____

Safety Rules

Read the following important rules for street safety. Follow these rules yourself and help others follow them, too.

1. Cross streets only at the corners.
2. Always look both ways before you cross the street.
3. Do not cross the street when the light is red.
   Wait until the light turns to green.
4. Do not walk between parked cars.
5. Always walk on the left side of the road, facing the cars.
6. Stop, look, and listen before you cross the railroad tracks.
   Be sure no train is coming.
7. Do not ride your bicycle on the sidewalk.
8. Help little children cross the street safely.
9. Do not get into a car with a stranger.
10. Find a police officer when you see trouble.

A. Finish each rule with the right word or words.

1. Cross only at _____.

2. _____, _____, and _____
   before you cross the railroad tracks.

3. Never get into a car with a _____.

4. Don't ride your bicycle on the _____.

5. Walk on the _____ side of the road, _____
   the cars.

6. When you see trouble, you should find a _____.

7. Before you cross the street, you should look _____ ways.

Application of reading and comprehension skills in a health context

Name _____

B. Finish each idea in your own words.

1. A police officer is someone who _____

_____.

2. A stranger is someone _____.

3. A red light means _____.

4. A green light means _____.

C. Think about these questions. Write answers for two of them.
   Why should you walk on the left side of the road, facing the cars?
   Why shouldn't you walk between parked cars?
   Why should you stop, look, and listen before you cross the railroad tracks?
   Why shouldn't you ride your bicycle on the sidewalk?

1. _____

_____

_____

_____

_____

2. _____

_____

_____

_____

_____

Application of thinking and writing skills in a health context

Antonyms

Name _____

An antonym is a word that has the opposite meaning of another word.	early - late

Read the words in each box below. Draw a line to match each word with its antonym (opposite).

large	old	few	many	slow	hot
young	weak	off	after	cold	fast
strong	small	before	on	over	under

save	bumpy	always	fair	day	night
smooth	spend	unfair	dry	yes	no
early	late	wet	never	frown	smile

Read the list of words below. Then read the sentences that follow. Write the word from the list that is an antonym (opposite) for the underlined word in each sentence.

| light | unkind | shut | shout |
| false | to | down | awake |

1. This letter is <u>from</u> Uncle Todd. _____*to*_____

2. I was <u>asleep</u> when Grandfather called. _____

3. Is this living room always so <u>dark</u>? _____

4. Please help me <u>open</u> this heavy door. _____

5. I will <u>whisper</u> the clue to you. _____

6. Is the answer to this question <u>true</u>? _____

7. Please walk <u>up</u> the steps with me. _____

8. Writing that letter was <u>kind</u>. _____

Synonyms

Name _____

A synonym is a word that has the same or nearly the same meaning as another word.

gift - present

Read the words in each box below. Draw a line to match each word with its synonym (word that has the same meaning).

talk	sad	hurt	quick
unhappy	speak	gift	present
small	little	fast	harm

listen	hurry		
rush	hear		
nice	kind		

glad	path	big	tell
forest	happy	say	large
trail	woods	pretty	beautiful

clean	yell
breeze	wind
shout	wash

Read the list of words below. Then read the sentences that follow. Write the word from the list that is a synonym (word that has the same meaning) for the underlined word in each sentence.

nice	cool	run	noisy
crowd	strength	sofa	soil

1. Carmen and Jimmy are sitting on the <u>couch</u>. _____sofa_____

2. There was a <u>mob</u> of people in the store. _____

3. Because it is <u>chilly</u> outside, I will wear a sweater. _____

4. Does Kenny have the <u>power</u> to lift that load? _____

5. Would your uncle like to <u>jog</u> with us? _____

6. It was <u>kind</u> of Carly to show me this book. _____

7. I woke up when I heard the <u>loud</u> horn. _____

8. Do you have enough <u>dirt</u> for that plant? _____

Identifying synonyms

Antonyms and Synonyms

Name _____

Read the words below. Circle the two words in each row that are antonyms (opposites).

1.	shiny	(large)	(small)	red	round
2.	fair	happy	little	sad	new
3.	cooked	yes	save	raw	slow
4.	nice	hot	tall	rich	poor
5.	cost	sink	send	float	grow
6.	mix	play	sold	sweet	bought

Read each sentence and the words beside it. Complete each sentence by writing the word that is a synonym (word that has the same meaning) for the word shown below the blank.

1. I will try not to ___*harm*___ the plants when I walk through the garden. (hurt)

   harm
   water

2. My _____ and I like to eat lunch together. (pals)

   aunt
   friends

3. This map shows where my _____ is. (street)

   road
   home

4. I knew she was happy by the _____ on her face. (grin)

   smile
   look

5. I made a _____ for Timmy's birthday. (present)

   cake
   gift

6. Does Carl know how to _____ a flat tire? (fix)

   remove
   repair

Identifying antonyms and synonyms

Antonyms and Synonyms

Name _____

Read each pair of sentences. In the blanks, write a pair of antonyms (opposites) from the sentences.

1. My father sold his old car last week.   *sold*

    I bought some paper for my art class.   *bought*

2. My basket is full of shiny red apples.   _____

    The empty shoe boxes are on the steps.   _____

3. We will be riding over a bumpy road.   _____

    The lake looks smooth this morning.   _____

4. Whisper the clue to your partner.   _____

    I heard you shout my name.   _____

Read each pair of sentences. In the blanks, write a pair of synonyms (words that have the same meaning) from the sentences.

1. What kind of present should I make for him?   *present*

    I saved my money to buy her a birthday gift.   *gift*

2. The school is near the city park.   _____

    Does your aunt live close to my friend's home?   _____

3. The teacher read the story to the class.   _____

    Would you like to hear a tale about a rabbit?   _____

4. If we hurry to the school, we can see the show. _____

    Because we were running out of time, we had to rush. _____

Antonyms and Synonyms

Name _____

Read the list of words below. Then read the sentences that follow. Write the word from the list that is an antonym (opposite) for the underlined word in each sentence.

never	float	late
strong	save	bought

1. I would like to <u>spend</u> some money this year.   *save*

2. Am I here too <u>early</u> to see the show? _____

3. Jake <u>always</u> brings his lunch from home. _____

4. The toy boat will <u>sink</u> when you put it in the water. _____

5. Running races has made my legs feel <u>weak</u>. _____

6. I <u>sold</u> baskets of flowers at the market. _____

Read the list of words below. Then read the sentences that follow. Write the word from the list that is a synonym (word that has the same meaning) for the underlined word in each sentence.

unhappy	cool	glad
present	path	pretty

1. I felt <u>sad</u> when my friend moved.   *unhappy*

2. The colored lights of the city look <u>beautiful</u>. _____

3. He made the painting as a <u>gift</u> for his uncle. _____

4. The wind makes me feel <u>chilly</u>. _____

5. I am <u>happy</u> that you could be with us today. _____

6. This <u>trail</u> leads to some picnic tables. _____

Assessment of identifying antonyms and synonyms in context

Homophones

Name _____

| Homophones are words that sound the same but have different spellings and different meanings. | would - wood |

Read the words. Draw a line to match each word with its homophone (word that sounds the same).

your	tow		night	knight		week	hear
toe	you're		knew	tale		here	sent
wait	weight		tail	new		cent	pale
too	sale		deer	dear		pail	weak
sail	two		maid	made		sea	see

Read each pair of sentences. In the blanks, write a pair of homophones (words that sound the same) from the sentences.

1. The book you want is on the right side of the shelf.

    Please write a letter to me soon.

    right

    write

2. My nose always gets sunburned when I'm at the beach.

    Edward knows the way to the new classroom.

    _____

    _____

3. Where can I buy some fishing line for my new rod?

    We went by the street where you used to live.

    _____

    _____

4. There is a big knot in that jump rope.

    Penny will not be running in the next race.

    _____

    _____

5. Before I bake bread, I must buy some flour.

    The flower will look nice in this tall yellow vase.

    _____

    _____

Homographs

Name _____

Homographs are words that have the same spelling but different meanings. Sometimes they are pronounced differently.

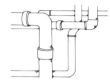

Those old pipes are made of **lead.**

Jack will **lead** the band.

Read each pair of sentences and circle the homographs (words that have the same spelling). Then draw a line from each sentence to the picture it tells about.

Connie will show us how to (wind) the clock.

The (wind) made the trees bend near the water.

I could feel the tree's rough bark.

The dog will bark when it sees you.

In the play, he must slowly bow to the queen.

Debbie tied a large bow onto the birthday gift.

Please tear the paper into two pieces.

A tiny tear fell from the baby's eye.

Jack will close the door of the car.

Annie stood close to the basketball hoop.

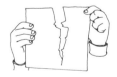

154

Identifying homographs; Determining meanings of homographs

Homophones and Homographs

Name _____

Read the words below. Circle the two words in each row that are homophones (words that sound the same).

1. been	(bear)	bake	(bare)	bale
2. beat	beak	bead	beet	bean
3. sink	cent	seem	center	scent
4. I	I've	eye	egg	elf
5. send	sea	see	sell	seat
6. heat	head	he	heal	heel

Read the homographs (words that have the same spelling) and their meanings below. Then read the sentences that follow. In each sentence, decide the meaning of the underlined homograph. Write the letter of the correct meaning in the blank.

lead
A. a heavy metal
B. to show the way

tear
A. to rip
B. a drop of water from the eye

close
A. to shut
B. near

1. The pipes in the old building are made of <u>lead</u>. _a_

2. Did I see a <u>tear</u> fall from your eye? _____

3. Russell stood <u>close</u> to his sister. _____

4. Who will <u>lead</u> us to the lake? _____

5. Please <u>close</u> the book when you are done reading the chapter. _____

6. Use the edge of the box to <u>tear</u> the wrapping paper. _____

Homophones and Homographs

Name _____

Read each pair of sentences. In the blanks, write a pair of homophones (words that sound the same) from the sentences.

1. I knew you would like to go walking through the city.   *knew*

   The tall building you see on this street is new.   *new*

2. Please meet me at the school lunchroom.   _____

   What kind of meat should I use in the soup?   _____

3. Carry the water in a little pail.   _____

   When I was sick, my face looked pale.   _____

4. You may use this oar in the rowboat.   _____

   Come to my house before or after lunch.   _____

5. I will be sailing for eight days.   _____

   The puppy ate all of its food today.   _____

Read the list of homographs (words that have the same spelling) below. Then read each pair of meanings that follows. Write the homograph from the list that matches both meanings.

wind	bark	close	tear	bow	lead

1. A. to bend the head or body   B. a knot made of ribbon   *bow*

2. A. to shut   B. near   _____

3. A. moving air   B. to turn or tighten   _____

4. A. water from the eye   B. to rip   _____

Review of identifying homophones; Determining meanings of homographs

Homophones and Homographs

Name _____

Read each pair of sentences. In the blanks, write a pair of homophones (words that sound the same) from the sentences.

1. The cut will heal quickly if it is kept clean.   *heal*

    My left shoe needs a new heel.   *heel*

2. She knew the answer to the question.   _____

    I found the new book on the top of the bookshelf.   _____

3. I rode to the woods on a brown pony.   _____

    Which road leads to the shopping center?   _____

4. The bear cubs in the zoo are so playful.   _____

    I walked in the sand in my bare feet.   _____

Read the homographs (words that have the same spelling) and their meanings below. Then read the sentences that follow. In each sentence, decide the meaning of the underlined homograph. Write the letter of the correct meaning in the blank.

wind
A. moving air
B. to turn or twist

bow
A. to bend the head or body
B. a knot made of ribbon

tear
A. to rip
B. a drop of water from the eye

1. You need to <u>wind</u> the key on that toy to make it work. *B*

2. Please put a yellow <u>bow</u> on that gift. ____

3. How did you <u>tear</u> your shirt? ____

4. The <u>wind</u> blew the leaves across the lawn. ____

Alphabetical Order

Name _____

You can put words in alphabetical order by looking at the first letter of each word. If the first letters of the words are the same, look at the second letters. If the second letters of the words are the same, look at the third letters.

dr**a**nk
dr**i**ve
dr**u**m

Read the lists of words. Number each list of words in alphabetical order.

List 1		List 2		List 3		List 4	
nail	_1_	price	___	clean	___	bring	___
nut	___	paint	___	city	___	blink	___
nine	___	pink	___	crown	___	broke	___
next	___	put	___	call	___	black	___
night	___	plum	___	coin	___	bread	___
noise	___	pond	___	cent	___	brush	___

Read the groups of words. Write each group of words in alphabetical order.

cream   crumb   cry   hide   home   heat   shelf   shine   shoe
    cross   crack   hall   hunt   shut   sharp

1. ___*crack*___   1. _____   1. _____

2. _____   2. _____   2. _____

3. _____   3. _____   3. _____

4. _____   4. _____   4. _____

5. _____   5. _____   5. _____

Alphabetizing by second and third letters

Guide Words

Name _____

The two words at the top of a dictionary page are called guide words. The first guide word is the same as the first word listed on the page. The second guide word is the same as the last word listed on the page. To find a word in the dictionary, decide if it comes in alphabetical order between the guide words on a page. If it does, you will find the word on that page.

Read each pair of guide words and the words that are listed below them. Circle the four words in each list that could be found on a page that has those guide words.

draw / foil	**melt / pony**	**boat / cone**
dime	past	crown
(drink)	open	bride
(face)	match	cloud
from	prize	call
(dust)	must	chain
(fire)	nine	cut

get / heavy	**rose / stand**	**two / wrote**
grow	rich	tractor
happy	slide	turtle
house	rush	under
icy	scarf	voice
give	some	world
goat	return	wind

Guide Words

Name _____

Read the six pairs of guide words and their dictionary page numbers. Then read the lists of words that follow. Write the page number on which each list word would be found in the dictionary.

apple / **bend**—p. 6   **both** / **bunch**—p. 8   **flight** / **give**—p. 26
glove / **happy**—p. 28   **roar** / **send**—p. 46   **sink** / **use**—p. 48

1. as   *p.6*

2. smell   _____

3. gaze   _____

4. bright   _____

5. breeze   _____

6. goat   _____

7. sand   _____

8. grown   _____

9. band   _____

10. speak   _____

11. base   _____

12. those   _____

13. branch   _____

14. geese   _____

15. rust   _____

16. brown   _____

17. art   _____

18. grape   _____

19. rug   _____

20. fresh   _____

21. bark   _____

22. sold   _____

23. rule   _____

24. guess   _____

Using guide words

Guide Words

Name _____

Read the lists of words below. Then read the guide words that follow. Write each list word below the correct pair of guide words. Then number each list of words to show how they would be listed in alphabetical order.

bench	cane	lunch	change	must
leave	ashes	my	born	city
buy	make	oak	law	barn
noise	nice	answer	chew	lime

1. above / broke

bench　　　 4

_____ ___

_____ ___

_____ ___

_____ ___

2. butter / corn

_____ ___

_____ ___

_____ ___

_____ ___

_____ ___

3. lamb / mice

_____ ___

_____ ___

_____ ___

_____ ___

4. mountain / old

_____ ___

_____ ___

_____ ___

_____ ___

Guide Words

Name _____

Read each pair of guide words and the words that are listed below them. Circle the four words in each list that could be found on a page that has those guide words.

held / ink	**jeep / leave**	**mist / nine**	**seat / such**
hall	large	monkey	shelf
(hide)	jail	march	south
(ice)	join	name	spare
(horse)	judge	melt	science
(howl)	June	myself	swing
itself	lift	neat	smoke

Read the four pairs of guide words and their dictionary page numbers. Then read the lists of words that follow. Write the page number on which each list word would be found in the dictionary.

above / are—p. 1   **arm / blue**—p. 2
both / child—p. 5   **cord / dime**—p. 7

1. ate   *p. 2*   8. always _____   15. dawn _____

2. add _____   9. bush _____   16. bunk _____

3. cost _____   10. air _____   17. aunt _____

4. brick _____   11. desk _____   18. chest _____

5. awake _____   12. angry _____   19. curl _____

6. being _____   13. apple _____   20. cent _____

7. animal _____   14. base _____   21. creek _____

Guide Words

Name _____

Read the lists of words below. Then read the guide words that follow. Write each list word below the correct pair of guide words. Then number each list of words to show how they would be listed in alphabetical order.

knee	heat	valley	idea	twelve
high	upon	listen	its	ice
uncle	jam	lace	jelly	job
lead	lump	hope	join	us

1. harm / inch

high   *2*

_____ ___

_____ ___

_____ ___

_____ ___

2. is / kept

_____ ___

_____ ___

_____ ___

_____ ___

_____ ___

3. kind / mercy

_____ ___

_____ ___

_____ ___

_____ ___

_____ ___

4. turn / village

_____ ___

_____ ___

_____ ___

_____ ___

_____ ___

Weather

Everyone talks about the weather, but no one does anything about it. Have you ever heard this saying? There's not much anyone *can* do about the weather. Would you like to have a picnic or go swimming? Do you want to go ice skating or ride your sled? The weather may decide what you can do.

Hot and Cold

In many places, it is hot in the summer. In the winter, it is cold. In the spring and fall, it may be warm on some days and cool on others. Knowing if it will be hot, warm, cool, or cold can help you decide how to dress and what kind of work or play you can do.

Wind

Air that moves sideways is called wind. A wind that blows from the north is cold, and a wind that blows from the south may be warm. The speed of the wind can change the weather.

Clouds

The clouds in the sky can also change the weather. There are different kinds of clouds. Many people can tell from the kind of clouds in the sky what the weather is going to be like. Some clouds mean rain; other clouds mean fair weather.

1. Check the word that tells the main idea.

_____ picnics   _____ weather   _____ clouds

2. Check each group of words that tells something that can change the weather.

_____ the speed of the wind

_____ the kind of clothes you wear

_____ the kind of clouds in the sky

Application of reading and comprehension skills in a science context

Name _____

3. Check the two sentences in which *wind* sounds the same.

_____ The wind blew my father's hat across the street.

_____ The wind howled loudly throughout the snowstorm.

_____ Please wind the clock before you go to bed tonight.

4. Check the two sentences in which *fair* has the same meaning.

_____ We had a wonderful time at the state fair this summer.

_____ The weather has been fair for three days in a row.

_____ I like to work in the garden when the weather is fair.

5. Tell how the weather might keep you from going to school.

_____

_____

6. Tell about some plans you made that were changed by the weather. What were the plans? What was the weather like? How did you change your plans because of the weather?

_____

_____

_____

_____

_____

_____

Application of thinking and writing skills in a science context

Sounds and Letters

fan

r**a**ke

tr**ai**n

j**ar**

auto

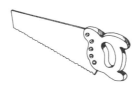

s**aw**

h**ay**

car

cent

chair

du**ck**

bed

b**ea**n

br**ea**d

bee

eight

fern

n**ew**s

goat

pa**ge**

Sounds and Letters

 lau**gh**

 b**i**b

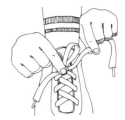 k**ite**

 t**ie**

 sh**ie**ld

 b**ir**d

 **kn**ot

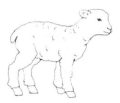 la**mb**

 ri**ng**

 t**o**p

 c**oa**t

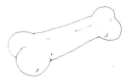 b**o**ne

 c**oi**n

 m**oo**n

 b**oo**k

 h**or**n

 cl**ou**d

 d**ou**ghnut

 t**ou**ch

 s**ou**p

Sounds and Letters

 wind**ow**

 **c**ow

 **toy**s

 ele**ph**ant

 **sc**issors

 **sh**oe

 **th**in

 **thr**ee

 **c**u**p**

 t**u**b**e**

 b**ur**n

 wheel

 **wr**ite

 fl**y**

 pon**y**

Beginning Sounds

Name

Read the words and name the pictures. Circle the word that names each picture.

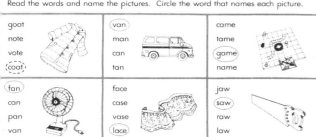

goat		van		came	
note		man		tame	
vote		can		(game)	
(coat)		tan		name	
(fan)		face		jaw	
can		case		(saw)	
pan		vase		raw	
van		(lace)		law	

Read the sentences. Complete the unfinished word in each sentence by writing the beginning consonant. The word you form must make sense in the sentence.

1. Please _j_oin us when we go camping next weekend.

2. You can _r_ead the map to see where we are going.

3. We will begin our trip in the _m_orning.

4. It will not take us long to set up the _t_ents when we get to the park.

5. When we get to the lake, we will fly _k_ites.

6. We may be able to go _b_ike riding.

7. When it is dark, we will build a _f_ire.

8. I will teach you how to sing a new _s_ong.

9. Will you say "_y_es" and come with us?

Beginning Sounds

Words to use: tunnel, map, vegetable, camera, desk, pitcher, log, sixteen, garage, needle, carrot, wolf, ribbon, comb, fan, zoo

Name

Look at the pictures. Write the letter or letters that stand for the beginning sound of each picture name.

_f_ork	_n_ail	_w_ink
_z_ipper	_qu_een	_h_ose

Read each sentence and the word beside it. In each line, change the first letter of the word in dark print to form a new word that will make sense in the sentence. Write the word in the blank.

1. I went to a pet show at the school last _night_. **might**

2. I have never seen so many cats and _dogs_. **hogs**

3. One boy had a _talking_ bird. **walking**

4. A small boy brought a basket that held three _kittens_. **mittens**

5. Another girl had a tank filled with _fish_. **wish**

6. I even saw a girl showing a pet _pig_. **big**

7. The _best_ pets were given prizes. **west**

8. Picking the winners must have been a hard _job_. **rob**

Ending Sounds

Name

Read the words and name the pictures. Circle the word that names each picture.

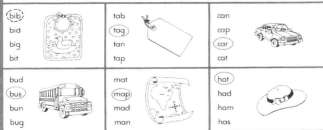

(bib)		tab		can	
bid		(tag)		cap	
big		tan		(car)	
bit		tap		cat	
bud		mat		(hat)	
(bus)		(map)		had	
bun		mad		ham	
bug		man		has	

Read the sentences. Complete the unfinished word in each sentence by writing the ending consonant. The word you form must make sense in the sentence.

1. Let me tell you what I di_d_ last week.

2. I too_k_ my first airplane ride over the city.

3. My ride was one afternoon after schoo_l_.

4. A friend of my da_d_ flew the small plane.

5. From the air I could see the tall buildings on my stree_t_.

6. Each car and bu_s_ that I saw looked like a little toy.

7. I could see the playground and the roo_f_ of our school.

8. Seeing the city from the air was a lot of fu_n_.

Ending Sounds

Words to use: bean, mix, chin, tool, boot, dig, cloud, pail, cup

Name

Name the pictures. Write the letter that stands for the ending sound of each picture name.

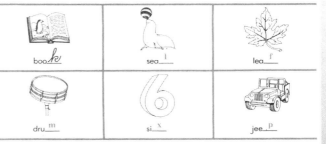

boo_k_	sea_l_	lea_f_
dru_m_	si_x_	jee_p_

Read each sentence and the word beside it. In each line, change the last letter of the word in dark print to form a new word that will make sense in the sentence. Write the word in the blank.

1. It is not easy to give my little _dog_ a bath. **dot**

2. I fill a big round _tub_ with soap and warm water. **tug**

3. When my dog hears the water running, she hides under

   my _bed_. **beg**

4. _Then_ I try to get my dog into the water. **Them**

5. The dog splashes me and gets me as _wet_ as she is. **web**

6. Her _fur_ looks clean when I am done. **fun**

7. Before I know it, my dog is in the _mud_ again! **mug**

Beginning and Ending Sounds

PROGRESS CHECK ✓

Name _____

Name the pictures. Write the letters that stand for the consonant sounds of each picture name.

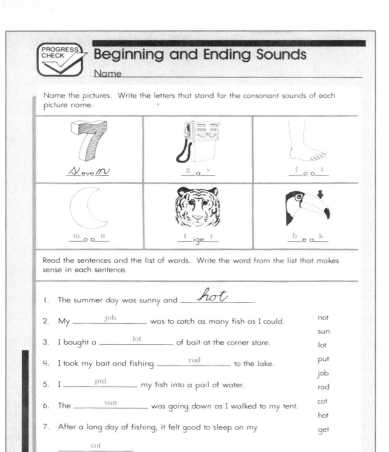

s_eve_n   g_a_s   f_o o_t

m_o o_n   t_ige_r   b_e a_k

Read the sentences and the list of words. Write the word from the list that makes sense in each sentence.

1. The summer day was sunny and __*hot*__
2. My __job__ was to catch as many fish as I could.
3. I bought a __lot__ of bait at the corner store.
4. I took my bait and fishing __rod__ to the lake.
5. I __put__ my fish into a pail of water.
6. The __sun__ was going down as I walked to my tent.
7. After a long day of fishing, it felt good to sleep on my __cot__

not
sun
lot
put
job
rod
cot
hot
get

Assessment of sound-symbol association of initial and final consonants; Words containing initial and final consonants in context   9

Short Vowels

Name _____

Read the words and name the pictures. Circle the word that names each picture.

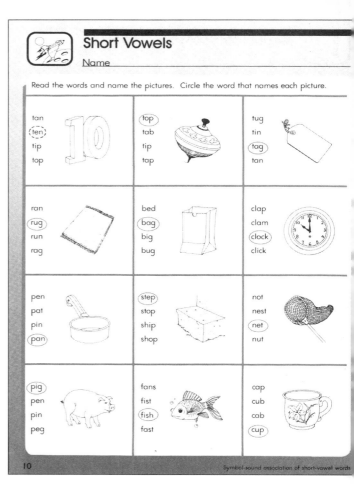

tan / (ten) / tip / top	(top) / tab / tip / tap	tug / tin / (tag) / tan
ran / (rug) / run / rag	bed / (bag) / big / bug	clap / clam / (clock) / click
pen / pat / pin / (pan)	(step) / stop / ship / shop	not / nest / (net) / nut
(pig) / pen / pin / peg	fans / fist / (fish) / fast	cap / cub / cab / (cup)

10   Symbol-sound association of short-vowel words

Short Vowels

Words to use: man, jet, tan, pen, hog, fox, nut, log, run, tip, pit, hug, pin

Name _____

Name the pictures. Write the letter that stands for the vowel sound of each picture name.

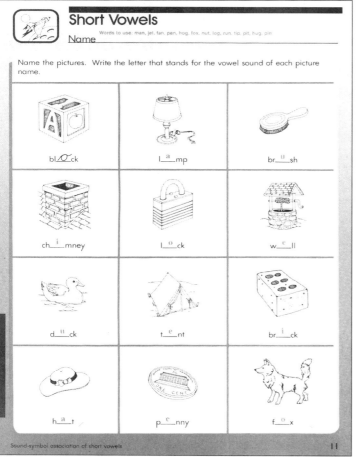

bl_a_ck   l_a_mp   br_u_sh

ch_i_mney   l_o_ck   w_e_ll

d_u_ck   t_e_nt   br_i_ck

h_a_t   p_e_nny   f_o_x

Sound-symbol association of short vowels   11

Short Vowels

Name _____

Read the words and name the pictures. Circle the word that names each picture.

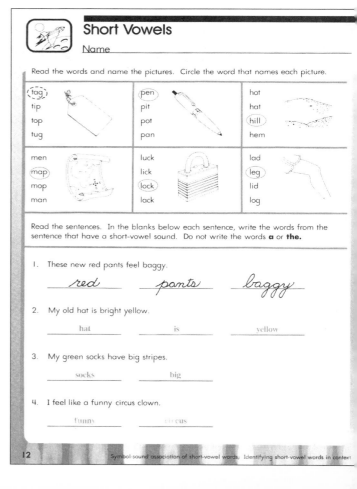

| (tag) / tip / top / tug | (pen) / pit / pot / pan | hot / hat / (hill) / hem |
| men / (map) / mop / man | luck / lick / (lock) / lack | lad / (leg) / lid / log |

Read the sentences. In the blanks below each sentence, write the words from the sentence that have a short-vowel sound. Do not write the words **a** or **the.**

1. These new red pants feel baggy.

   __*red*__   __*pants*__   __*baggy*__

2. My old hat is bright yellow.

   __hat__   __is__   __yellow__

3. My green socks have big stripes.

   __socks__   __big__

4. I feel like a funny circus clown.

   __funny__   __circus__

12   Symbol-sound association of short-vowel words; Identifying short-vowel words in context

Short Vowels

Name

Read each set of sentences and its list of words. Write the word from the list that makes sense in each sentence.

1. Many of my school friends started a ___ *club* ___

2. We like to go hiking and ___ *camping* ___ at nearby places.

3. Tomorrow we ___ *plan* ___ to go on a hike through the woods.

4. You can meet ___ *us* ___ early in the morning.

5. You will get hungry, so remember to bring a ___ *lunch* ___

6. If you need a backpack, I can ___ *lend* ___ you one.

7. My father ___ *can* ___ take us to the park.

club
us
luck
camping
can
plan
stamp
lend
lunch

8. Jack's mom will ___ *bring* ___ us home.

9. I hope we have a ___ *sunny* ___ day.

10. We'll talk about the hike the ___ *next* ___ time we meet.

11. Carlos ___ *will* ___ show us his pictures.

12. Sally might bring the ___ *rocks* ___ and leaves she finds.

13. Kim will ___ *tell* ___ us about other parks.

14. We may want to talk about taking a camping ___ *trip* ___

15. When the morning is over, we can eat a ___ *snack* ___

jump
will
next
bring
rocks
snack
pick
sunny
tell
trip

Short Vowels

Name

Read the sentences. Complete the unfinished word in each sentence by writing the missing vowel. The word you form must make sense in the sentence.

1. I visited the farm animals l_a_st week.

2. I w_e_nt inside the big red barn with my friend Maria.

3. There I saw a large p_i_g sleeping in the corner of a pen.

4. Many young pigs ran around in another large p_e_n.

5. I could tell they liked running in the m_u_d.

6. It was fun to sp_e_nd time looking at the pigs.

7. Outside I saw a b_i_g horse.

8. My friend showed me how it could tr_o_t around the barn.

9. She also showed me how to br_u_sh the horse's coat.

10. The horse l_e_t me pet its nose.

11. Its nose felt warm and s_o_ft.

12. Now I w_i_sh I had a horse of my own.

13. I can't have one in my c_i_ty apartment.

14. So, I'll go b_a_ck to visit the farm again.

Long Vowels

Name

Read the words and look at the pictures. Circle the word that tells about each picture.

(bike) bake bite base	cage code cone cane	mile mole (mule) male
rope rake (robe) ride	like lane lake (line)	(nose) nine note nice
cove (cane) cave cone	rage robe rode (rake)	cage (cube) cape cute
dime (dive) date dune	time (tube) tide tune	hope (hive) home hike

---

Long Vowels

Name

Read the words and look at the pictures. Circle the word that tells about each picture.

rise rope (rose) ripe	(skate) slide snake slope	(home) hide hive hose
time (tape) take tide	fine fake (five) face 	time tile tube (tune)

Read the sentences. In the blanks below each sentence, write the words from the sentence that have a long-vowel sound. Do not write the words **a** or **the**.

1. I like visiting different places.

   ___ *I* ___   ___ *like* ___   ___ *places* ___

2. Last June I visited another state with a friend.

   ___ June ___   ___ I ___   ___ state ___

3. We went swimming and rode bikes in a park.

   ___ We ___   ___ rode ___   ___ bikes ___

4. I wrote a tune about our summer trip.

   ___ I ___   ___ wrote ___   ___ tune ___

Long Vowels

Name _____
Words to use: cake, rice, lake, rose, cave, dime, tube, stone, ice, cage, vine, line, note, cane, robe, mule, cone, nine, tube

Look at the pictures. Write the letter or letters that stand for the vowel sound in each picture name.

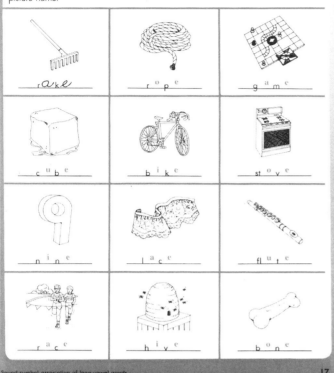

r_a_k_e_	r__o_p__e_	g__a_m__e_
c__u_b__e_	b__i_k__e_	st__o_v__e_
n__i_n__e_	l__a_c__e_	fl__u_t__e_
r__a_c__e_	h__i_v__e_	b__o_n__e_

Sound-symbol association of long-vowel words   17

Long Vowels

Name _____

Read the sentences. Complete the unfinished word in each sentence by writing the missing vowel. The word you form must make sense in the sentence.

1. It was l_a_te one night when I heard the noise.

2. I had been sleeping, and the noise w_o_ke me.

3. I didn't have a clock, so I'm not sure what t_i_me it was.

4. The wh_i_te light of the moon lit my bedroom.

5. I h_a_te to say that I was feeling afraid.

6. Again I heard the s_a_me sound.

7. I must have looked p_a_le as I sat up in bed.

8. I felt myself starting to sh_a_ke.

9. I remember telling myself to be br_a_ve.

10. I got out of bed and put on a warm r_o_be.

11. I called my cat's n_a_me.

12. A sound c_a_me from the toy box in a corner of my room.

13. Guess who had found a new place to h_i_de?

14. I felt myself begin to sm_i_le.

15. The cat looked c_u_te as she jumped out of the toy box when I opened it.

18   Long-vowel words in context

OLD and IND

Name _____

The letter **o** followed by **ld** usually stands for the long-**o** sound. The letter **i** followed by **nd** usually stands for the long-**i** sound.

cold
kind

Read each sentence and words beside it. Write the word that makes sense in each sentence.

1. Did you get _cold_ while you were waiting for the bus?

   cone
   cold
   cot

2. When I got a new bike, I _sold_ my old one.

   sold
   soak
   sock

3. Would you _mind_ going shopping with me?

   mix
   mine
   mind

4. Little children like to _hold_ our puppy.

   hold
   home
   hoe

5. Please keep your reading papers in this _folder_.

   colder
   folder
   older

6. Were you able to _find_ the button you lost?

   find
   fin
   fine

7. What _kind_ of eggs shall I cook today?

   kind
   king
   kite

8. Linc said to my teacher, "I am feeling _fine_."

   find
   fin
   fine

9. Were you at home when Luis _told_ you the news?

   fold
   told
   cold

Words containing old and ind in context   19

OLD and IND

Name _____

Read the sentences and the list of words. Write the word from the list that makes sense in each sentence.

1. It was _kind_ of you to walk my dog.

2. The shop on the corner _sold_ balloons and kites.

3. The workers will _grind_ the meat while you wait.

4. I'm having trouble _finding_ my math paper.

5. Do you know where we can buy a candle _holder_ to set on our new table?

6. Visiting Denny was the _kindest_ thing you could do for him.

7. After we do the wash, we must _fold_ the clothes.

8. His ride through the snowstorm showed that the prince was _bold_.

9. Would you _mind_ if I bring my brother and sister with me?

10. The park worker _told_ us about the animals that live in the woods.

11. Seeing-eye dogs are used to lead _blind_ persons.

12. I keep all of my school papers in a large _folder_.

13. Which of the five bicycles is the _oldest_?

fold
finding
told
blind
grind
holder
oldest
kind
bold
sold
mind
kindest
folder

20   Words containing old and ind in context

172

Long Vowels

Name _____

Read each set of sentences and its list of words. Write the word from the list that makes sense in each sentence.

1. Last spring I __*wrote*__ a letter to my aunt.
2. I wanted to visit her __home__ for a week.
3. She said it would be __nice__ for me to visit.
4. One night I flew there in a huge __plane__.
5. We were lucky that we didn't have one __cold__ day.
6. We spent a lot of time __outside__.
7. I wanted to __find__ some rocks to take to school.
8. I found many __pine__ cones, too.

wrote
cold
nice
flute
outside
home
find
plane
told
pine

1. One day I helped my aunt by using a __rake__ in the garden.
2. For fun, I jumped into a __pile__ of straw.
3. Each evening, I fed the __cute__ calf.
4. Before the sun went down, I would __ride__ the pony.
5. After dinner, my uncle would play a __tune__ for us on his flute.
6. He showed me how he reads the __es__ of each song.

pile
cute
grind
rake
notes
sold
tune
ride

Assessment of long-vowel words in context 21

Short and Long Vowels

Words to use: tape, mice, fish, clock, cold, bike, tug, bib, cent, hole

Name _____

Name the pictures. Write the letter or letters that stand for the vowel sound of each picture name.

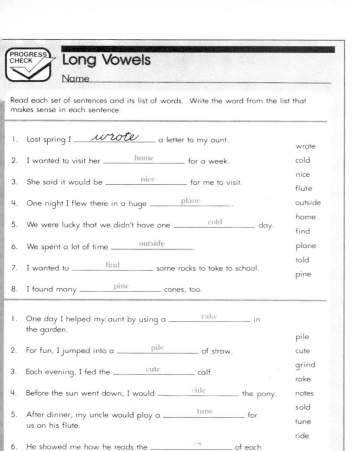

f __i__ ve | l __a__ ke | s __u__ n
b __e__ d | r __o__ pe | f __a__ n
r __a__ ke | g __o__ ld | d __i__ me
fl __u__ te | p __i__ g | t __o__ p

22   Sound-symbol association of short- and long-vowel words

Short and Long Vowels

Name _____

Read the sentences. Complete the unfinished word in each sentence by writing the missing vowel or vowels. The word you form must make sense in the sentence.

1. The family garden is in b __a__ ck of the house.
2. Every spring, I h __e__ lp my mother plant the seeds.
3. First we use a shovel to d __i__ g up the soil.
4. We use a r __a__ k __e__ to make the soil smooth.
5. Then the seeds are planted in n __i__ n __e__ straight rows.
6. The summer s __u__ n helps the plants grow.
7. I pick every ripe green bean that I can f __i__ nd.
8. We begin going to the market in J __u__ n __e__.
9. We t __a__ k __e__ a lot of the food that grew in our garden.
10. The food is s __o__ ld from the back of our new truck.
11. I put each person's food in a paper b __a__ g.
12. Sometimes I s __i__ t and watch the people.
13. The bright shining sun makes me h __o__ t.
14. It makes me want to j __u__ mp into a lake.
15. That's just what my d __a__ d lets me do after we leave the market.

Short- and long-vowel words in context 23

Short and Long Vowels

Name _____

Read each sentence and the words beside it. Write the word that makes sense in each sentence.

1. We should __*stop*__ at Abby's costume shop. | stop / step / stone
2. She will __let__ us try on some clothes. | let / led / leg
3. You might enjoy looking at the __masks__. | must / masks / most
4. You'll also like trying on each hat you __find__. | fin / find / fine
5. I __like__ to dress up as a big white bunny. | like / lake / line
6. Dressing like a football player is __fun__, too. | fun / fan / fin
7. My brother looks __cute__ in an elf costume. | cut / cute / cube
8. If you want to fool people, wear a curly __wig__. | wag / wig / wide
9. Wouldn't you look strange in long __pink__ hair? | pink / pine / pin
10. If you want to look like a clown, wear a shiny red __nose__. | nice / nose / name

24   Short- and long-vowel words in context

Short and Long Vowels

Name _____

Read each set of sentences and its list of words. Write the word from the list that makes sense in each sentence.

1. When we _**camp**_, I like to hike in the nearby woods.

2. I pick up each pine _**cone**_ I see.

3. I sometimes find a bird's _**nest**_ that is filled with eggs.

4. A small animal sometimes comes out of a _**hole**_ in the ground.

5. I carefully watch where I _**step**_.

6. I want the animals to be _**safe**_.

7. Someday I will _**write**_ a story about the things I have seen in the woods.

write
camp
step
ship
cone
mind
safe
nest
hole

---

1. My grandfather's house is near the bank of a _**pond**_.

2. I feed the _**ducks**_ when I visit.

3. I like to watch them _**swim**_ around.

4. To get sun, they sit on a flat _**rock**_.

5. All the ducks march in a _**line**_.

6. They look so _**cute**_.

7. I _**wish**_ I lived near a pond as Grandfather does.

wish
line
hold
pond
cute
ducks
swim
rock
stamp

Short and Long Vowels

Name _____

Read each sentence and the words beside it. Write the word that makes sense in each sentence.

1. Randy will be _**ten**_ years old on his birthday.

ten
tan
ton

2. We are beginning to _**plan**_ a surprise party.

plan
plane
plant

3. Kristy will _**tell**_ our friends about the party.

tall
talk
tell

4. Bobby and Sandy can _**bake**_ a cake.

back
bake
base

5. Jeff will teach us a new _**kind**_ of game.

king
kind
kick

6. Let's make a _**huge**_ sign that says, "Happy Birthday."

hug
huge
hum

7. When it's time, Randy's grandmother will _**send**_ him to the store.

sand
send
sent

8. We will _**hide**_ behind the chairs in his house.

hid
hide
hive

9. Jill will begin the birthday _**tune**_.

tune
tube
tub

10. I _**hope**_ Randy will be surprised!

hope
hop
home

Hard and Soft C and G

Name _____

The letters **c** or **g** followed by **e, i,** or **y** usually stand for their soft sounds, as in **cent** and **page.** The letters **c** or **g** followed by any other letters usually stand for their hard sounds, as in **cat** and **wagon.**

 cent (soft **c**)   pa**ge** (soft **g**)

Read the words and name the pictures. Draw a line from each word to the picture it names.

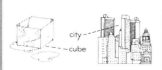 city — cube

 game — stage

 giraffe — garden

 card — celery

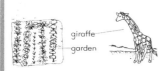 pig — cage

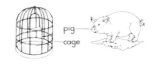 calf — face

---

Hard and Soft C and G

Name _____

Read the lists of words. Notice the sound that **c** or **g** stands for in each word. Then write each word under the correct heading.

cent (soft **c**)   pa**ge** (soft **g**)

contest	goose	place	dragon	goat
price	cow	stage	cabin	calf
fence	guess	cab	gentle	judge
bridge	center	wig	edge	excited

Words may be listed in any order.

Hard **c** as in **cat**	Soft **c** as in **cent**
contest	price
cow	fence
cab	center
cabin	place
calf	excited

Hard **g** as in **wagon**	Soft **g** as in **page**
goose	bridge
guess	stage
wig	gentle
dragon	edge
goat	judge

174

Hard and Soft C and G

Name _____

Read the sentences. In the blanks below each sentence, write the words from the sentence that have soft **c** or **g**.

cent (soft **c**)   pa**ge** (soft **g**)

1. Gail moved to a city with a well-known bridge.

   city   *bridge*

2. The picture on that page shows a gentle giant.

   page   gentle   giant

3. The judge will hear the first case in this place.

   judge   place

Read the sentences. In the blanks below each sentence, write the words from the sentence that have hard **c** or **g**.

1. Can you get the cat before it runs under the fence?

   Can   *get*   *cat*

2. We raced to catch the goat in the garden.

   catch   goat   garden

3. The cow was excited when it got outside the gate.

   cow   got   gate

Identifying hard- and soft-c and hard- and soft-g words in context   29

Hard and Soft C and G

Name _____

Read the sentences and the words beside them. Write the word that makes sense in each sentence.

1. Please sign this birthday *card* . — city / cost / card

2. We can send it to our friend in the ___city___ . — city / cost / card

3. Read the words on the first ___page___ of this book. — cage / page / game

4. They tell you how to play a running ___game___ . — cage / page / game

5. Would you like a ___slice___ of wheat bread? — cup / cent / slice

6. Should I fill your ___cup___ with milk? — cup / cent / slice

7. The park is near the ___bridge___ that crosses the stream. — bridge / car / garden

8. Wing likes to look at the flower ___garden___ there. — bridge / car / garden

9. When the play begins, I am standing on the ___stage___ . — wagon / gentle / stage

10. She will sing a very ___gentle___ song. — wagon / gentle / stage

11. Did you like the animal shows in the ___circus___ ? — price / circus / cute

12. I thought the monkeys were ___cute___ . — price / circus / cute

13. Do you like the taste of ___rice___ ? — center / cook / rice

14. I can ___cook___ some for you to try. — center / cook / rice

30   Review of hard- and soft-c and hard- and soft-g words in context

---

Hard and Soft C and G

Name _____

Read each sentence. Circle the word **hard** or **soft** to tell the kind of sound the **c** or **g** in dark print stands for. Remember: **Cent** and **page** have soft sounds. **Cat** and **wagon** have hard sounds.

1. Where will the cooking **c**ontest be held? — (hard) / soft

2. There is a bicycle shop in the **c**enter of the town. — hard / (soft)

3. My make-believe story is about an unhappy fro**g**. — (hard) / soft

4. What kind of **g**ame should we play? — (hard) / soft

5. After he ran two miles his fa**c**e was red. — hard / (soft)

6. Will you help me choose a **c**andle? — (hard) / soft

7. Her father bought her a new silver bra**c**elet. — hard / (soft)

8. Lin wore a long black wi**g** at the costume party. — (hard) / soft

9. Do you know the pri**c**e of that football shirt? — hard / (soft)

10. The **g**iraffe has a long neck. — hard / (soft)

11. Stand away from the ed**g**e of the cliff. — hard / (soft)

Assessment of hard- and soft-c and hard and soft-g words   31

Two-Letter Blends

Name _____
Words to use: twist, swim, snack, speed, sting, smell, clap, flip, plug, glide, blink, sleep, broke, fresh, trick, drip, grin, cream, prize, square

In some words, one consonant follows another consonant. To say these words, blend the sounds of the two consonants together.

stop   **tw**in
play   **squ**irrel
green

Read the words and look at the pictures. Circle the word that tells about each picture.

(crib) / trip / grin / drip	clock / float / (block) / glove	trap / (snap) / slap / clap
grown / brown / frown / (crown)	stone / (smoke) / spoke / slope	dry / (cry) / fry / pry
flow / glow / slow / (snow)	black / clam / (flag) / glass	spot / slide / stir / (squirrel)
twice / twin / (twine) / twig	flame / plane / slate / (plate)	draw / (tray) / gray / crab

32   Symbol-sound association of words containing tw, s, l, and r blends

175

Two-Letter Blends

Name _____

Words to use: broom, frost, twin, snap, plum, blink, gray, train

Read each sentence and the words beside it. Write the word that makes sense in each sentence.

1. I like to roller _____*skate*_____ outdoors.		state skate slate
2. I _____*start*_____ at my house and skate to the park.		smart start scarf
3. If I think I'm going to fall, I hold onto a _____*tree*_____.		free tree glee
4. I am careful not to trip on each _____*crack*_____ of the sidewalk.		crack track black
5. The smooth path in the park helps me to _____*glide*_____.		glide twin slid
6. My arms _____*swing*_____ as I skate along the path.		sting swing skip
7. The soft _____*breeze*_____ feels good in my hair.		breeze freeze green
8. I sometimes _____*dream*_____ about flying through the air.		great twenty dream
9. I meet two people on the path and _____*squeeze*_____ between them.		sweater squeeze speech
10. After skating I am tired, but I feel _____*great*_____!		great cream treat

Words containing *tw, s, l,* and *r* blends in context   33

Two-Letter Blends

Name _____

Words to use: twenty, swell, spoke, spark, stamp, smile, cloud, flower, plate, squeeze, drink, prize, gray

Read the sentences. Complete the unfinished word in each sentence by writing the missing blend. Choose from the following blends: **sw, cl, fl, br, fr, sq.** The word you form must make sense in the sentence.

1. Please help me _*cl*_ean my dirty bedroom.
2. I will pick up the clothes from the _*fl*_oor.
3. Would you _*sw*_eep the floor with this broom?
4. My brother's toy _*sq*_uirrel is under the bed.
5. Here is the _*br*_ush that I thought was lost.
6. Now I can walk _*fr*_om place to place without tripping over things!

Read the sentences. Complete the unfinished word in each sentence by writing the missing blend. Choose from the following blends: **tw, sc, sn, sp, st, gl, sl.** The word you form must make sense in the sentence.

1. Grandfather will _*sc*_old me if I get up.
2. He said I should try to _*sl*_eep.
3. I guess he heard me _*sn*_eezing this morning.
4. My _*tw*_in sister had a cold before I did.
5. She had to _*sp*_end two days in bed last weekend.
6. She told me that Grandfather can also tell a good _*st*_ory any time of day.
7. I am _*gl*_ad that Grandfather is here.

34   Words containing *tw, s, l,* and *r* blends in context

Two-Letter Blends

Name _____

Read each clue. Complete the word beside it to form a word that matches the clue. Choose from the following blends: **tw, sl, sm, st, sw.** You may use a blend more than once.

1. something you need to mail a letter — _*st*_amp
2. the number before thirteen — _*tw*_elve
3. a toy used to ride on snow — _*sl*_ed
4. something you can do in a pool or lake — _*sw*_im
5. to mix food — _*st*_ir
6. something you do when you are happy — _*sm*_ile

Read each clue. Complete the word beside it to form a word that matches the clue. Choose from the following blends: **bl, fl, br, gr, tr, cr, sq.**

1. the color of the sky — _*bl*_ue
2. a path — _*tr*_ail
3. a kind of fruit that grows on a vine — _*gr*_ape
4. something that hangs on a pole — _*fl*_ag
5. something that can be made into toast — _*br*_ead
6. a shape that has four sides of the same length — _*sq*_uare
7. a loud noise — _*cr*_ash

Review of words containing *tw, s, l,* and *r* blends   35

Three-Letter Blends

Name _____

In some words, the letter **s** is followed by two other consonants. To say these words, blend the sound of **s** with the sounds of the consonants that follow.

spring
scream
split
strip

Read the words and look at the pictures. Circle the word that tells about each picture.

split (string) spring strip	strange sprang (splash) scratch	stream spread (screw) street
split (splinter) strip strike	street scream stream (spread)	(spray) scratch strange sprang
screech (spread) stream (street)	splash (scratch) straight sprang	spread scream (stream) street
sprout (strong) scrap stroke	spray scrape (straw) splash	strange (scrape) splash sprang

36   Symbol-sound association of words containing three-letter blends: *spr, scr, spl, str*

Three-Letter Blends

Name: _____ Words to use: spray, spread, sprout, sprain, scrap, screen, split, stripe, straight, screech, scratch, splash, strong, splinter, strip

Read each sentence and the words beside it. Write the word that makes sense in each sentence.

1. What a _____strange_____ day I've had today!

   scratch
   strange
   sprang

2. I _____split_____ a seam in my yellow shirt.

   strike
   split
   strip

3. I _____spread_____ butter on my hand instead of on the toast.

   stream
   spread
   scream

4. My best friend _____sprained_____ his leg when we were playing.

   stranger
   sprained
   screamed

5. I forgot to get a _____straw_____ for my milk when I went through the lunch line.

   strange
   straw
   straight

6. The _____strap_____ on my only backpack broke.

   splash
   strap
   scratch

7. I ran into the _____screen_____ door.

   stream
   screen
   spread

8. I got a _____splinter_____ in my right hand.

   splinter
   strip
   strike

9. A car _____splashed_____ water on me.

   scraped
   splashed
   scratched

10. I think I'll go _____straight_____ to bed when I get home!

    spray
    scratch
    straight

ords containing three-letter blends in context: spr, scr, spl, str   37

Three-Letter Blends

Name: _____

Read the sentences. Complete the unfinished word in each sentence by writing the missing blend. Choose from the following blends: **spr, scr, spl, str.** You may use a blend more than once. The word you form must make sense in the sentence.

1. Would you like to fix _____scr_____ambled eggs for Grandmother?

2. Can Brenda swim _____str_____aight across the deep end of the pool?

3. Try not to make a big _____spl_____ash when you dive.

4. I used the hose to _____spr_____ay water for the children.

5. Last spring I helped put a new _____scr_____een in my window.

6. How did Jan _____spr_____ain her arm?

7. We plan to plant some flowers next _____spr_____ing.

8. Before winter, we _____spl_____it wood to burn in our fireplace.

9. Before we begin painting the house, we must _____scr_____ape off the old paint.

10. Scott let out a loud _____scr_____eam when you frightened him.

11. Listen to that _____str_____ange noise.

12. Is Allan _____str_____ong enough to lift this box?

13. The first time Billy was up to bat, he got a _____str_____ike.

14. How did you get that _____spl_____inter in your finger?

15. Are there any fish in that shallow _____str_____eam?

38   Words containing three-letter blends in context: spr, scr, spl, str

---

Three-Letter Blends

Name: _____

Read each clue. Complete the word beside it to form a word that matches the clue. Choose from the following blends: **spr, scr, spl, str.** You may use a blend more than once.

1. to hurt an arm or leg by twisting it   _____spr_____ain

2. not curved   _____str_____aight

3. something cats do with their claws   _____scr_____atch

4. a wide brook   _____str_____eam

5. to hurt the skin on a knee   _____scr_____ape

6. to wash with a brush   _____scr_____ub

7. what water does when you jump into a pool   _____spl_____ashes

8. something found in a barn   _____str_____aw

9. a time of year when flowers bloom outdoors   _____spr_____ing

10. a tiny piece of wood   _____spl_____inter

11. another name for a road   _____str_____eet

12. to yell in a high voice   _____scr_____eam

13. to put butter on bread   _____spr_____ead

14. to break something apart   _____spl_____it

15. to scatter tiny drops of water   _____spr_____ay

view of words containing three-letter blends: spr, scr, spl, str   39

Ending Blends

Name: _____ Words to use: grand, task, sort, sift, ask, desk, spend, mask, rent, bump, skirt, left, lift

At the end of some words two consonants appear together. To say these words, blend the sounds of the two consonants together.

la**st**	sta**mp**
ha**nd**	gi**ft**

Read the words and name the pictures. Circle the word that names each picture.

gasp (gift) golf gust	(cast) camp cent cost	soft sand (sink) sent
mast mist (mask) milk	pink (plant) pump pant	bump (belt) built best
rent (raft) ramp rest	bank bent bend (band)	(lamp) left lump lift
stamp stand (stump) stunt	(shelf) shirt shift skunk	skunk skirt shift (shirt)

40   Symbol-sound association of words containing final blends

Ending Blends

Name _____

Words to use: camp, past, blend, dent, lend, bank, lump, art

Read each sentence and the words beside it. Write the word that makes sense in each sentence.

1.	You need to put on old pants and a _shirt_.	shift / shirt / shelf
2.	I want you to go with me to see what's _left_ in the old barn.	lift / left / lamp
3.	You can _help_ me open the heavy sliding door.	honk / help / hand
4.	I'll see if I can find a _lamp_ to give us some light.	land / lamp / last
5.	Look at the rusty tools on this _shelf_.	short / shelf / shift
6.	Do you think Grandfather used this tool to _plant_ seeds?	plant / part / paint
7.	She wants to know what kind of bird _built_ that nest.	belt / built / bold
8.	We will have to _ask_ our teacher.	ask / ant / and
9.	I can _send_ him a letter tonight.	send / sent / self
10.	Let's go to the old _fort_ on our next visit.	fast / fort / first

---

Ending Blends

Name _____

Words to use: hand, paint, mint, list, round, wink, gulf, hurt, link, stand

Complete the unfinished word in each sentence by writing the missing blends. Choose from the following blends: **lf, lt, st, mp, nk, rt, ft, nd, nt, sk.** You may use a blend more than once. The word you form must make sense in the sentence.

1. My friends met our family at the city airpo_rt_.
2. A strong wi_nd_ was blowing.
3. We ran to put the bags into the tru_nk_ of the car.
4. We stayed at my friend's home because we fe_lt_ it was too cold to camp.

5. First I put a funny ma_sk_ on my face.
6. Next I'll put on a wig made of so_ft_ yellow yarn.
7. I will wear a bright red shi_rt_ and baggy blue pants.
8. Then I'll be ready to go to work in the circus te_nt_.

9. Most of the books that tell how the old fo_rt_ was built have been sold.
10. There aren't many left on the she_lf_.
11. People must like the pictures drawn by the book's arti_st_.
12. They sit at the de_sk_ in the bookstore and look at the books.

13. Please put a sta_mp_ on this letter.
14. I will se_nd_ it to Mom after we go swimming.
15. She will want to know about the ra_ft_ ride we took on the river.

REVIEW

Ending Blends

Name _____

Read each clue. Complete the word beside it to form a word that matches the clue. Choose from the following blends: **st, sk, nd, nk, nt, mp, lf, lt, rt, ft.** You may use a blend more than once.

1.	a small lake	po_nd_
2.	to spread color with a brush	pai_nt_
3.	a tiny, make-believe person	e_lf_
4.	what is left of a tree after it has been cut down	stu_mp_
5.	a place to save money	ba_nk_
6.	the part of the body that pumps blood	hea_rt_
7.	the plaster covering on a broken arm or leg	ca_st_
8.	a present	gi_ft_
9.	the opposite of right	le_ft_
10.	something found at a beach	sa_nd_
11.	a place for airplanes	airpo_rt_
12.	a penny	ce_nt_
13.	a group of people who play songs while marching	ba_nd_
14.	a table used for writing or studying	de_sk_
15.	a young male horse	co_lt_

PROGRESS CHECK ✓

Blends

Name _____

Read each set of sentences and its list of words. Write the word from the list that makes sense in each sentence.

1. Patty walks to the _pond_ in the park.
2. Her dog runs _past_ her.
3. The dog likes to _splash_ water on itself.
4. Patty calls, and the dog runs _straight_ to her.
5. Patty _squeals_ as her dog jumps up.
6. She throws a _stick_ into the air.
7. That dog likes to _play_ "catch."

play / straight / squeals / stick / pond / splash / draw / past / plan

1. One day last week I was standing in _front_ of the house.
2. I saw something _start_ to move.
3. What was that _strange_ animal?
4. I moved slowly and tried to get _close_ to it.
5. I was surprised to see a _skunk_!
6. I've always been afraid of their _smell_.
7. "Oh, _please_ don't let it spray me," I thought.
8. I was lucky that I didn't _scream_.

close / skunk / smell / free / front / scream / block / strange / start / please

178

Page 45

Silent Consonants: *KN, WR,* and *SC*

Name _____

In some words, two consonants together stand for one sound.
The letters **kn** usually stand for the sound of **n**, as in **knot**.
The letters **wr** usually stand for the sound of **r**, as in **write**.
The letters **sc** sometimes stand for the sound of **s**, as in **scissors**.

knot
write
scissors

Look at the pictures. Write the letters that stand for the beginning sound of each picture name.

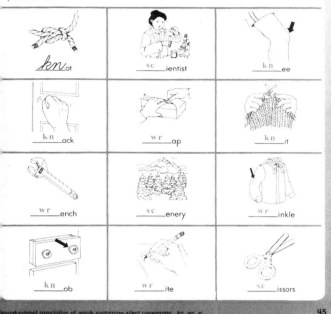

*kn*ot   __s c__ientist   __k n__ee

__k n__ock   __w r__ap   __k n__it

__w r__ench   __s c__enery   __w r__inkle

__k n__ob   __w r__ite   __s c__issors

Sound-symbol association of words containing silent consonants: kn, wr, sc   45

Page 46

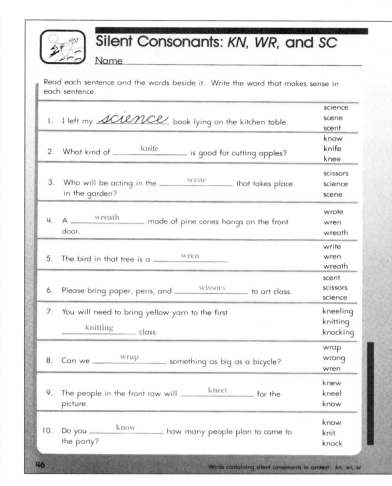

Silent Consonants: *KN, WR,* and *SC*

Name _____

Read each sentence and the words beside it. Write the word that makes sense in each sentence.

1. I left my _science_ book lying on the kitchen table.
   — science / scene / scent

2. What kind of ___knife___ is good for cutting apples?
   — know / knife / knee

3. Who will be acting in the ___scene___ that takes place in the garden?
   — scissors / science / scene

4. A ___wreath___ made of pine cones hangs on the front door.
   — wrote / wren / wreath

5. The bird in that tree is a ___wren___.
   — write / wren / wreath

6. Please bring paper, pens, and ___scissors___ to art class.
   — scent / scissors / science

7. You will need to bring yellow yarn to the first ___knitting___ class.
   — kneeling / knitting / knocking

8. Can we ___wrap___ something as big as a bicycle?
   — wrap / wrong / wren

9. The people in the front row will ___kneel___ for the picture.
   — knew / kneel / know

10. Do you ___know___ how many people plan to come to the party?
    — know / knit / knock

46   Words containing silent consonants in context: kn, wr, sc

---

Page 47

Silent Consonants: *KN, WR,* and *SC*

Name _____

Read each set of sentences and its list of words. Write the word from the list that makes sense in each sentence.

1. Arthur helped his brother get the _knot_ out of his shoelace.

2. When I finish ___wrapping___ this box, we can go to the party.

3. My father ___knew___ your mother when they were both children.

4. The ___scientist___ won a prize for her work.

5. I am afraid that I'll ___wrinkle___ my costume if I sit down.

6. Are those ___scissors___ sharp enough to cut this heavy paper?

knew
wrinkle
knot
scissors
wrong
wrapping
scientist
knowing

---

1. Was your mom able to put a new ___knob___ on the door?

2. Is that a new watch I see on your ___wrist___?

3. Last week I bought a pair of ___knee___ socks to go with my new skirt.

4. I have always liked smelling the ___scent___ of roses.

5. Jennifer thought she heard a ___knock___ at the door.

6. Did Cathy see the second ___scene___ of the play?

scene
wrench
knob
knock
wrist
knee
wrong
scent

Words containing silent consonants in context: kn, wr, sc   47

Page 48

Silent Consonants: *CK, MB,* and *GH*

Name _____

In some words, two consonants together stand for one sound.
The letters **ck** usually stand for the sound of **k**, as in **duck**.
The letters **mb** usually stand for the sound of **m**, as in **lamb**. The letters **gh** are usually silent, as in **night**.

du**ck**
la**mb**
ni**gh**t

Read the list of words below. Then look at the pictures. Write a word from the list that tells about each picture.

truck   eight   comb   climb   block
brick   light   clock   thumb

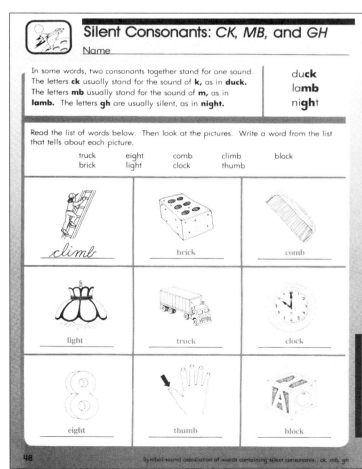

climb   brick   comb

light   truck   clock

eight   thumb   block

48   Symbol-sound association of words containing silent consonants: ck, mb, gh

---

Silent Consonants: CK, MB, and GH

Name _____

Read each sentence and the words beside it. Write the word that makes sense in each sentence.

1. The little _chicks_ followed their mother.		sticks / chicks / thick
2. My teacher _taught_ Allen how to play the drums.		eight / taught / sight
3. Andrew will _comb_ his hair before his picture is taken.		comb / climb / thumb
4. How many times can you run around the _track_?		pack / track / back
5. Our family _might_ take a trip this summer.		might / sight / right
6. Before the grass is cut, we must walk around the yard and pick up each _stick_.		thick / stick / lick
7. Each fire fighter must _climb_ the ladder.		thumb / climb / comb
8. We ate dinner on our plane _flight_ to the city.		bright / fright / flight
9. The children have fun with these building _blocks_.		blocks / socks / locks
10. Did you hurt your _thumb_ with the hammer?		climb / thumb / comb

---

Silent Consonants: CK, MB, and GH

Name _____

Read each set of sentences and its list of words. Write the word from the list that makes sense in each sentence.

1. I was able to hold a _lamb_ when I visited the zoo.	bright
2. The new house is made of _bricks_.	sock
3. The little child covered with mud was quite a _sight_.	night / truck
4. Do I have a hole in the toe of my _sock_?	lamb
5. Are you seven or _eight_ years old?	thumb
6. Jess plans on _climbing_ that mountain.	eight / climbing
7. Is the sun always so _bright_ in this window?	sight
8. The dump _truck_ can carry a heavy load.	bricks

1. In the winter, the birds eat the bread _crumbs_ we give them.	comb
2. He was surprised when he _caught_ the ball.	light / check
3. We cannot ride our bicycles until it is _light_ outside.	block
4. The gift was a brush and _comb_ set.	high
5. How _high_ is the new downtown building?	crumbs
6. Did you _check_ to see that the lights are off?	sigh / climb
7. We heard them _sigh_ when the race was over.	caught

Silent Consonants

Name _____

Read each clue. Write **kn**, **wr**, **sc**, **ck**, **mb**, or **gh** to complete the word that matches the clue.

1. a time to sleep	ni _gh_ t
2. painted scenes used in a play	_sc_ enery
3. the flying of a plane or a jet	fli _gh_ t
4. to make something with yarn	_kn_ it
5. the part of the arm near the hand	_wr_ ist
6. something used to make hair smooth	co _mb_
7. a baby sheep	la _mb_
8. the middle part of the leg	_kn_ ee
9. a stone	ro _ck_
10. to put words down on paper	_wr_ ite
11. not low	hi _gh_
12. something you do to get into a tree	cli _mb_
13. something a train moves on	tra _ck_
14. a tool used to tighten nuts and bolts	_wr_ ench
15. the smell of something	_sc_ ent

Silent Consonants

Name _____

Read the list of words below. Then read the sentences that follow. Write the word from the list that makes sense in each sentence.

crumbs	lock	knob	wrinkle	knock	science	wrap
quick	eight	scene	taught	thumb	straight	knew

1. If you _knock_ three times, we'll let you into the clubhouse.
2. She twisted the _knob_ to turn on the television.
3. Danny painted a beautiful _scene_ of the mountains.
4. If we are _quick_, we can catch the morning train.
5. Aunt Joyce knew we had been eating because there were _crumbs_ on the table.
6. Be careful not to _wrinkle_ your new shirt.
7. The children learned about plants in _science_ class.
8. The holes in the scissors are for your finger and your _thumb_.
9. Chee _taught_ his little sister how to tie her shoes.
10. What should Cindy use to _wrap_ the food for our lunches?
11. This bicycle path goes _straight_ through the city.
12. So far, we have only _eight_ persons playing on our team.
13. Be sure to _lock_ the car door before you go shopping.
14. I _knew_ you would like reading that book.

In some words, two vowels together stand for one vowel sound. The letters **ai** and **ay** usually stand for the long-**a** sound, as in **train** and **hay.** The letters **ei** sometimes stand for the long-**a** sound, as in **eight.**

tr**ai**n
h**ay**
eight

Read the words and look at the pictures. Circle the word that tells about each picture.

sail (train) say tray	tray (chain) train chair	say (sail) stay sprain
braid trail brain (tray)	drain (playground) paint daisy	(hay) chain hair claim
wail stay (weigh) sail	sail say stay (sleigh)	fail vein faint (veil)
sprain stay (spray) stain	pay pail (paint) play	weight (eight) sleigh weigh

Symbol-sound association of words containing vowel digraphs: *ai, ay, ei*   53

Read each sentence and words beside it. Write the word that makes sense in each sentence.

1. How long must we wait for the afternoon *train* ? — tray / tail / train

2. What kind of ___freight___ do trains and planes carry? — reigns / freight / sleigh

3. Can you teach me how to ___braid___ my hair? — braid / chain / grain

4. You can carry the dishes to the table on a ___tray___. — train / tray / tail

5. The nurse wrote my ___weight___ on a chart. — freight / weight / sleigh

6. Could you help me get the ___nail___ out of the board? — nail / sail / tail

7. The children liked the story about the well-known ___reindeer___ that could fly. — reindeer / freight / weight

8. Some people ___spray___ water on their plants. — say / straight / spray

9. Can you ___stay___ at my house when your family goes away? — stain / stay / sleigh

10. Do you know how to fix a bicycle ___chain___? — braid / chain / train

54   Words containing vowel digraphs in context: *ai, ay, ei*

Read the list of words below. Then read the sentences that follow. Write the word from the list that makes sense in each sentence.

weight	crayons	daisy	playground	aim
stay	trail	sleigh	mail	highway
neighbor	eighteen	way		

1. We count cars when our family drives on the ___highway___.

2. Who will pick up your ___mail___ at the post office when you are out of town?

3. You can score a point if you ___aim___ the basketball at the rim.

4. Growing flowers is something my ___neighbor___ does well.

5. If you walk on this dusty ___trail___, you will come to Oak Lake.

6. Where will you ___stay___ when you go on your trip to the city?

7. When it snows, Mrs. Bobbitt takes children on ___sleigh___ rides through the woods.

8. You can find scissors, paper, and many ___crayons___ in my desk.

9. If you want to play kickball, meet on the school ___playground___.

10. There are ___eighteen___ boys and girls in that club.

11. Yoko put a ___daisy___ in her hair.

12. Which ___way___ should I turn when I get to the school?

13. As I grow taller, I will gain ___weight___.

Words containing vowel digraphs in context: *ai, ay, ei*   55

In some words, two vowels together stand for one vowel sound. The letters **ee** usually stand for the long-**e** sound, as in **bee.** The letters **ea** can stand for the long-**e** sound, as in **bean** or the short-**e** sound, as in **bread.** The letters **oa** and **ow** often stand for the long-**o** sound, as in **coat** and **window.**

b**ee**
b**ea**n
br**ea**d
c**oa**t
wind**ow**

Read the words and name the pictures. Circle the word that names each picture.

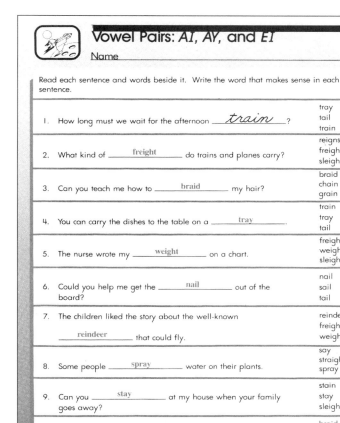

beak (bee) bow boat	green (goat) grow groan	bowl bread boat (beach)
seek sneak (snow) seat	head heat (heel) heavy	loaf (leaf) lean low
sheep (shadow) show sheet	bee beak (bread) beach	boat beat bean (bowl)
three (thread) throat throw	row read roast (road)	tea teeth (tree) treat

56   Symbol-sound association of words containing vowel digraphs: *ee, ea, oa, ow*

181

Vowel Pairs: *EE, EA, OA,* and *OW*

Name _____

Read each sentence and the words beside it. Write the word that makes sense in each sentence.

1. Do you know how to tie a ___*bow*___ ?

   bow
   beak
   bee

2. I fixed the ___wheel___ of my bicycle.

   wheat
   wheel
   week

3. Would you like some butter or jelly on your ___toast___ ?

   toast
   team
   teeth

4. You may have some eggs for ___breakfast___ .

   bread
   breakfast
   breath

5. Our basketball ___team___ works hard when it plays.

   team
   tow
   teen

6. Today we'll have ___cheese___ and crackers for our snack.

   cheek
   cheese
   cheap

7. The school nurse says I am very ___healthy___ .

   heats
   healthy
   heel

8. That dish can be cleaned with ___soap___ and water.

   soap
   seed
   seal

9. When my uncle sees me he always says, "My, how you've ___grown___ ."

   grown
   green
   greet

10. We will go swimming at the ___beach___ behind our neighbor's house.

    beak
    beach
    been

Vowel Pairs: *EE, EA, OA,* and *OW*

Name _____

Read the list of words below. Then read the sentences that follow. Write the word from the list that makes sense in each sentence.

need	teeth	heavy	show	bowl
reach	steep	float	goat	teacher
grow	meant	feather	roast	

1. Jane will be happy to ___*show*___ you her drawing.

2. We had fun feeding the playful ___goat___ at the zoo.

3. The chart on the classroom wall was made by the ___teacher___ .

4. We were careful when we climbed the ___steep___ hill.

5. The basket of apples was too ___heavy___ for me to carry.

6. Justin ___meant___ to call you this morning.

7. My little sister tried to ___reach___ the books on the highest shelf.

8. When we were in the swimming pool, my dad showed me how to ___float___ .

9. The dentist checks my ___teeth___ twice a year.

10. Will I ___need___ eggs to make the muffins?

11. Let's put the popcorn in this yellow ___bowl___ .

12. This daisy will ___grow___ to be as tall as the fence.

13. I found a bird's ___feather___ on the beach.

14. How long will it take to ___roast___ the meat in this oven?

Vowel Pairs: *EE, EA, OA,* and *OW*

Name _____

Read each sentence and look at the vowel pairs beside it. Write one of the vowel pairs to complete the unfinished word in each sentence. The word you form must make sense in the sentence.

1. Put on your heavy c___oa___t before we go outside.   oa, ea

2. I can hear the wind bl___ow___ing.   ee, ow

3. Let's walk on this winding r___oa___d that leads to the barn.   oa, ee

4. We will give the horse a tr___ea___t.   ea, ow

5. The horse likes to eat ___oa___ts from our hands.   ea, oa

6. Don't you think its fun to ___ow___n a horse?   ow, ee

1. It's always pl___ea___sant to think about a summer trip.   oa, ea

2. I like to dr___ea___m about the many places I want to visit.   ea, ow

3. Sometime I'd like to take a long b___oa___t trip so I could see the sights.   ea, oa

4. I have always m___ea___nt to plan a train trip to the West.   ow, ea

5. The train I want to ride would have a place for me to sl___ee___p.   ee, ow

---

Vowel Pairs: *OO, AU, AW,* and *EW*

Name _____

In some words, two vowels together stand for one sound. The letters **oo** can stand for the sound you hear in the middle of **moon** or **book**. The letters **au** usually stand for the sound you hear at the beginning of **auto**. The letters **aw** usually stand for the sound you hear at the end of **saw**. The letters **ew** usually stand for the sound you hear in the middle of **news**.

m**oo**n
b**oo**k
auto
s**aw**
n**ew**s

Read the words and look at the pictures. Circle the word that tells about each picture.

(book) boot blew broom	screw school (straw) spoon	(faucet) few fault flew
droop (draw) dew dawn	claw jaw (jewel) chew	(hook) haul hoop hood
food fool flew (foot)	lawn look (launch) law	(pool) straw paw spoon
saw (screw) soon straw	blew (boot) book brook	noon blew (news) book

182

Vowel Pairs: OO, AU, AW, and EW

Name _____

Read each sentence and the words beside it. Write the word that makes sense in each sentence.

1. The light of the ___moon___ was bright last night.

   mew
   moon
   moose

2. I believe there are a ___few___ tickets left for the show.

   fawn
   few
   fault

3. Patrick ___stood___ in the rain and waited for the bus.

   spoon
   scoop
   stood

4. We will get up at ___dawn___ to catch the early morning train.

   dawn
   dew
   draw

5. What kind of ___sauce___ should we make for the meat?

   sauce
   screw
   straw

6. Colleen ___drew___ a picture of the snowy mountains.

   dew
   drew
   droop

7. Does that ___rooster___ crow every morning?

   raccoon
   spoon
   rooster

8. The new speed ___law___ helps keep the highways safe.

   look
   launch
   law

9. Marty hit a fly ball, and Benny ___caught___ it.

   caught
   claw
   cause

10. Richard ___shook___ the coins out of his piggy bank.

    shook
    straw
    sauce

Vowel Pairs: OO, AU, AW, and EW

Name _____

Read the list of words below. Then read the sentences that follow. Write the word from the list that makes sense in each sentence.

cause	look	yawn	flew	daughter
hawk	few	kangaroo	hook	taught
tooth	drawings	spoon	grew	

1. The baby needs a ___spoon___ for the food.

2. His little sister just lost a front ___tooth___.

3. I ___yawn___ when I get up too early in the morning.

4. Martin likes to make ___drawings___ of birds and flowers.

5. Please hang your coat on the ___hook___ behind the door.

6. Can you tell me if that bird is a ___hawk___?

7. The princess is the ___daughter___ of the queen.

8. My aunt will ___look___ for a new car today.

9. My teacher ___taught___ me how to add numbers.

10. Do you have a ___few___ minutes to listen to my tape?

11. When my family visited the zoo, my brother wanted to see a baby ___kangaroo___ in its mother's pouch.

12. Do the fire fighters know the ___cause___ of the fire?

13. A hot-air balloon ___flew___ over the fairgrounds this morning.

14. The farmers ___grew___ more corn this year than last.

Vowel Pairs: OO, AU, AW, and EW

Name _____

Read each sentence and look at the vowel pairs beside it. Write one of the vowel pairs to complete the unfinished word in each sentence. The word you form must make sense in the sentence.

1. There is much to do after sch__oo__l.   oo, au

2. You may plan to play baseball on the front l__aw__n.   aw, ew

3. The swimming p__oo__l is open.   oo, au

4. You can check out a b__oo__k from the library.   oo, aw

5. You'll need to p__au__se and think about what you'd like to do.   au, oo

1. One day we got up at d__aw__n.   aw, oo

2. A f__ew__ of us quickly got dressed.   aw, ew

3. We had planned a walk in the w__oo__ds.   oo, au

4. Our leader had t__au__ght us about animal tracks.   oo, au

5. Before long, Danny s__aw__ some small tracks.   oo, aw

6. We were following a family of racc__oo__ns.   au, oo

Vowel Pairs

Name _____

Read the list of words below. Then read the sentences that follow. Write the word from the list that makes sense in each sentence.

| bread | train | stay | speak | steep | soon | keep |
| book | draw | few | jewel | own | road | drew |

1. I would like to make some ___bread___ for my neighbor.

2. Can you ___stay___ here awhile and help me bake a loaf?

3. I need a map that shows the ___road___ where the shops are.

4. Please ___draw___ the map with a marker on this sheet of paper.

5. Will you ___keep___ these tickets for me until I'm ready to go?

6. I will be taking a ___train___ ride into the city to see your daughter.

7. Nancy got a ___book___ from the library today.

8. Someday she would like to have her ___own___ set of books.

9. My aunt and uncle have a ___few___ horses and cows.

10. They will also have sheep at their ranch ___soon___.

11. Andrew ___drew___ a picture of a fancy crown.

12. A beautiful ___jewel___ was in the center of the crown.

13. Are you able to ___speak___ to the group at this week's meeting?

14. We would like to hear about the ___steep___ mountain you climbed.

Page 65

Vowel Pairs: IE

Name _____

Tie has the long-i sound spelled by the letters **ie**. **Shield** has the long-e sound spelled by the letters **ie**.

 t**ie**   sh**ie**ld

Read the words and look at the pictures. Circle the word that tells about each picture.

(tie) lie	die (pie)	lie (necktie)
field (lie) 	niece (movie)	chief (thief)
(field) movie 	die (chief)	piece (die)
(cookie) tie 	(piece) pie	field (shield)

Symbol-sound association of words containing *ie*   65

Page 66

Vowel Pairs: IE

Name _____

Read the list of words. Notice the sound that **ie** stands for in each word. Then write each word under the correct heading.

 t**ie**   sh**ie**ld

field	lie	niece	thief
necktie	pie	die	movie

Order of words may vary.

Long **i** as in **tie**	Long **e** as in **shield**
necktie	field
lie	niece
pie	thief
die	movie

Read the sentences. Complete each sentence by writing a word from the exercise above. The word you write must make sense in the sentence.

1. His __*necktie*__ matched the color of his jacket.
2. We like to pick wild flowers from the __field__ near our home.
3. Would you like to __lie__ down and rest?
4. Her family watched an exciting __movie__ about runners.
5. What made that plant __die__?
6. My __niece__ has a beautiful smile.
7. The __thief__ had taken the important papers.

66   Symbol-sound association of words containing *ie*; Words containing *ie* in context

Page 67

Vowel Pairs: IE

Name _____

Read the sentences and the list of words. Write the word from the list that makes sense in each sentence.

 t**ie**   sh**ie**ld

1. Mindy will __tie__ string around the box.
2. I would like to be the __chief__ of the fire fighters.
3. I __believe__ you can run the race faster than you ever have before.
4. Should my dad wear a __necktie__ tonight?
5. The grass will __die__ if it doesn't get enough water.
6. Have you ever told a __lie__?
7. May I have another __piece__ of paper?
8. The teacher showed a __movie__ after we talked about the city.
9. The police are looking for the __thief__ who ran out of the bank with the money.
10. I have been an aunt since my __niece__ Kris was born.
11. The team can play softball in that __field__.
12. Each knight in the painting is holding a heavy _____ shield

chief
shield
die
piece
niece
necktie
thief
lie
field
believe
movie
tie

Words containing *ie* in context   67

Page 68

Vowel Pairs: OU

Name _____

In some words, two vowels together stand for one vowel sound. The letters **ou** can stand for the vowel sounds you hear in **soup** and **should**.

s**ou**p   sh**ou**ld

Read the list of words. Notice the sound that **ou** stands for in each word. Write each word under the correct heading.

group	wouldn't	could	through	coupon
would	shouldn't	youth	couldn't	you

Order of words may vary.

ou as in **soup**	**ou** as in **should**
group	would
youth	wouldn't
through	shouldn't
coupon	could
you	couldn't

Read the sentences and the word choices. Circle the word that makes sense in each sentence.

1. Grandmother told me I (through, (should)) remember to wear my coat.
2. ((Wouldn't), Youth) it be nice to have a picture of that sunset?
3. We save money by using (should, (coupons)) when we shop.
4. A ((group), couldn't) of six children will play on each team.
5. Our teacher told us we (coupon, (could)) write a story.
6. What kind of (should, (soup)) do I smell cooking?
7. We will hike over the hill and ((would), through) the woods.

68   Symbol-sound association of words containing *ou*; Words containing *ou* in context

184

Vowel Pairs: OU

Name _____

In some words, two vowels together stand for one vowel sound. The letters **ou** can stand for the vowel sounds you hear in **touch** and **doughnut**.

| **tou**ch |
| **dou**ghnut |

Read the list of words. Notice the sound that **ou** stands for in each word. Write each word under the correct heading.

double   couple   dough   southern   shoulder
enough   although   young   though

Order of words may vary.

ou as in **touch**	**ou** as in **doughnut**
double	although
enough	dough
couple	though
young	shoulder
southern	

Read the sentences and the word choices. Circle the word that makes sense in each sentence.

1. Have you ever tasted bread ((dough) double) like this?
2. Debbie knows how to make whole wheat (double, (doughnuts)).
3. Would you like to visit my uncle in the ((country) couple)?
4. Jennie's ((cousin) though) can make flutes out of wood.
5. The player who made a ((touchdown), through) jumped up and down.
6. I put the backpack over my (southern, (shoulder)).
7. Do you have ((enough), although) wood to build a fire?

Vowel Pairs: OU

Name _____

Read the story. Circle each word that contains **ou.** Then answer the questions that follow. There are twenty-three words that contain **ou.**

Though we had never done it before, our youth group planned to make bread. We should have started with something easy, but we like bread! We went through the food store with many coupons, buying enough for an army.

Jan wanted us to get double of everything on our list. Doug had to carry a large bag of flour over his shoulder. The shopkeeper said it looked as if we were going to open a shop with all of the bread we planned to make.

The next day we all met at the home of Jan's cousin. Our plan was to first mix a little bit of the dough. We didn't have any trouble. Before long, we had baked a beautiful loaf of bread. We spent the rest of the day baking bread. By the time we were through, we had enough for each of us to take a loaf home.

I shared my bread with my family. My dad said, "The group you belong to is young, but they surely know how to bake." He should know. He ate five pieces!

Use the story to answer the questions.

1. What word from the first paragraph rhymes with **dough?** _*though*_
2. What kind of group baked the bread? _____ youth
3. What did the group take to the store in order to save money? _____ coupons
4. What word from the second paragraph means "twice as much"? _____ double
5. How did Doug carry the flour? _____ over his shoulder
6. What word from the third paragraph means "finished"? _____ through

---

Vowel Pairs

Name _____

Read the list of words below. Then read the sentences that follow. Write the word from the list that makes sense in each sentence.

necktie   field   dough   would   should
chief   enough   tie   believe
route   touch   movie   through

1. I have never worn a _*necktie*_ before.
2. Will you show me how to _____ tie _____ it?
3. What _____ would _____ I do without your help?
4. We can make this _____ dough _____ into bread or rolls.
5. There may be _____ enough _____ of the mix to make both.
6. Let's taste the bread as soon as we're _____ through _____ .
7. This is the _____ route _____ shown on the map that we should follow.
8. It will take us past a _____ field _____ of corn.
9. Can you _____ believe _____ that covered wagons once used this road?
10. Would you and your brother like to see a good _____ movie _____ ?
11. The show is about a well-known Indian _____ chief _____ .
12. The zoo worker said that some snakes _____ should _____ be fed every day.
13. She asked us if we'd like to _____ touch _____ the skin of a snake.

Two Sounds of Y

Name _____

When **y** comes at the end of a word that has no other vowel, the **y** usually stands for the long-**i** sound as in **fly**. When **y** comes at the end of a word that has another vowel, the **y** usually stands for the long-**e** sound as in **pony**.

fl**y**   pon**y**

Read the words and look at the pictures. Circle the word that tells about each picture.

fly (jelly)	spy (puppy)	carry (cry)
(dry) daisy	(fly) funny	fry (forty)
(sky) snowy	try (rainy)	funny (fry)
(daisy) dry	silly (sky)	(rocky) cry

Two Sounds of Y

Name _____

Read the words below. Write **long e** or **long i** next to each word to show the sound that **y** stands for.

fl**y**   pon**y**

1. fly	*long i*	7. stormy	long e
2. angry	long e	8. shy	long i
3. sixty	long e	9. lucky	long e
4. why	long i	10. fry	long i
5. dry	long i	11. empty	long e
6. thirsty	long e	12. cry	long i

Read the sentences and the word choices. Circle the word that makes sense in each sentence.

1. Tommy will (try, fry) to answer each of your questions.
2. Can you get me a (carry, copy) of the story you read to us today?
3. We can go sled riding on the first (sixty, snowy) day.
4. When I learned that my best friend was moving, I began to (dry, cry).
5. Should we buy a pack of twenty or (rainy, forty) paper plates for the party?
6. On the day we began our trip there wasn't a cloud in the (shy, sky).
7. Are those math books too (heavy, healthy) for you to carry?
8. I'd like to know (shy, why) the date of the football game was changed.

Two Sounds of Y

Name _____

Read the list of words. Notice the sound that **y** stands for in each word. Write each word under the correct heading.

fl**y**   pon**y**

try	sky	sixty	stormy	fry
cry	penny	rocky	shiny	shy

Long **i** as in **fly**	Long **e** as in **pony**
try	penny
cry	sixty
sky	rocky
fry	stormy
shy	shiny

Words may be listed in any order.

Read the sentences. Complete each sentence by writing a word from the exercise above. The word you write must make sense in the sentence.

1. Would you like to ___*try*___ to fly my new kite?
2. We climbed up the steep, ___rocky___ hillside.
3. Will that school bus hold more than ___sixty___ children?
4. Have you ever tried to count each star in the ___sky___ ?
5. Uncle Richard can bake or ___fry___ the fish in a pan for you.
6. Aunt Janie's new ___shiny___ bicycle is silver.

Vowel Pairs and Sounds of Y

PROGRESS CHECK

Name _____

Read the list of words below. Then read the sentences that follow. Write the word from the list that makes sense in each sentence.

try	taught	weight	raccoon	healthy
field	trail	cousin	cheese	straw
toast	chew	window	through	

1. We should ___*try*___ to get together to play basketball.
2. I would like two eggs and some ___toast___ with jam this morning.
3. The farmer carried a bale of ___straw___ into the barn.
4. The nurse always checks the baby's ___weight___ on the scales.
5. Dennis ___taught___ us how to use a rowboat.
6. What kind of ___cheese___ should I put on this sandwich?
7. Mandy's puppy likes to ___chew___ toy bones.
8. We can fly kites from the grassy ___field___.
9. Eating good food helps you stay ___healthy___.
10. I wish my ___cousin___ could go shopping with us.
11. Every year the hiking ___trail___ is used by many people.
12. I never rode ___through___ a tunnel.
13. If you look out this ___window___, you can see the lights of the city.
14. Did you see that ___raccoon___ walking on our picnic table?

Reading and Writing Wrap-Up

Name _____

City Workers

Many people in the city work to help us. They do things for us that we cannot do for ourselves.

Police

Police officers help us in many ways. They help people cross the street safely. They help little children find their way if they are lost. They find people who break the law. They make our cities safe to live in.

Mail Carriers

Mail carriers bring letters and newspapers to people's homes. They also bring books, toys, and clothes that we have sent away for. They do their work in sun, snow, rain, or wind.

Fire Fighters

Fire fighters are ready at all times to fight fires. They put out fires in homes and other buildings. They save people's lives. They go to schools to teach children about fire safety.

1. Check the answer that tells the main idea.

   _✓_ people who help us

   ____ what people can do to help the police

   ____ how to fight fires

2. Write two things that fire fighters do.

   They put out fires. They save people's lives. They teach children

   about fire safety. Other answers are also possible.

186

Name _____

3. Write the name of the worker under each picture.

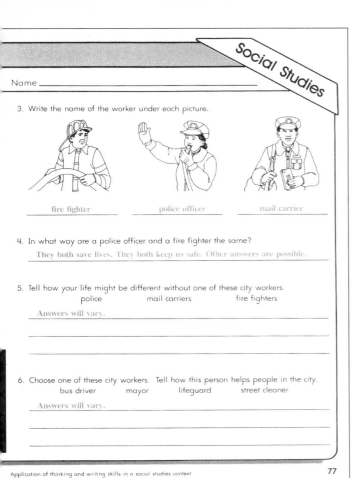

fire fighter   police officer   mail carrier

4. In what way are a police officer and a fire fighter the same?

They both save lives. They both keep us safe. Other answers are possible.

5. Tell how your life might be different without one of these city workers.

    police   mail carriers   fire fighters

Answers will vary.

_____

_____

6. Choose one of these city workers. Tell how this person helps people in the city.

    bus driver   mayor   lifeguard   street cleaner

Answers will vary.

_____

_____

Application of thinking and writing skills in a social studies context   77

Consonant Pairs

Words to use: shelf, shield, child, thorn, whistle, chin, shop, shark, sheet

Name _____

Two consonants together can stand for one sound. Some consonants that stand for one sound are **sh, ch, th,** and **wh.** At the beginning of some words, three consonants together stand for a special sound as in **three.**

shoe	**wh**eel
chair	**thr**ee
thin	

Name the pictures. Write the letters that stand for the beginning sound in each picture name.

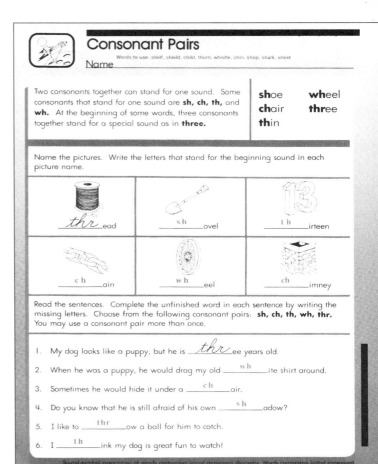

_thr_ead	s h ovel	t h irteen
c h ain	w h eel	ch imney

Read the sentences. Complete the unfinished word in each sentence by writing the missing letters. Choose from the following consonant pairs: **sh, ch, th, wh, thr.** You may use a consonant pair more than once.

1. My dog looks like a puppy, but he is _thr_ee years old.

2. When he was a puppy, he would drag my old ___w h___ite shirt around.

3. Sometimes he would hide it under a ___c h___air.

4. Do you know that he is still afraid of his own ___s h___adow?

5. I like to ___thr___ow a ball for him to catch.

6. I ___t h___ink my dog is great fun to watch!

78   Sound-symbol association of words containing initial consonant digraphs; Words containing initial consonant digraphs in context. sh, ch, th, wh, thr

---

Consonant Pairs

Name _____

Read each sentence and the words beside it. Write the word that makes sense in each sentence.

1. If you get some _thread_, I will fix your coat.
    cheese / thread / shed

2. I always lay my glasses on this ___shelf___.
    three / shelf / check

3. In art class, we form clay into many different ___shapes___
    shapes / change / thanks

4. The police believe that a ___thief___ tried to break into the bank.
    thief / whip / chin

5. I will read my book ___while___ you talk to the man who works in the children's library.
    child / while / shield

6. Are there any sea animals bigger than a ___whale___?
    chain / shake / whale

7. Is there a ___chance___ that you'll be able to go swimming with me?
    shark / than / chance

8. The queen sat on a ___throne___ to receive her crown.
    shook / throne / choke

9. Our group would like to ___thank___ you for your help with the play.
    thank / chain / shadow

10. Before we build a fire, let's have the ___chimney___ cleaned.
    thirteen / chimney / whistle

Words containing initial consonant digraphs in context: sh, ch, th, wh, thr   79

Ending Consonant Pairs

Name _____

At the end of a word, two or three consonants together can stand for one sound. Some consonants that stand for one sound are **sh, ch, tch, th,** and **ng.**

wi**sh**	wi**th**
ea**ch**	ri**ng**
ca**tch**	

Name the pictures. Write the letters that stand for the ending sound in each picture name.

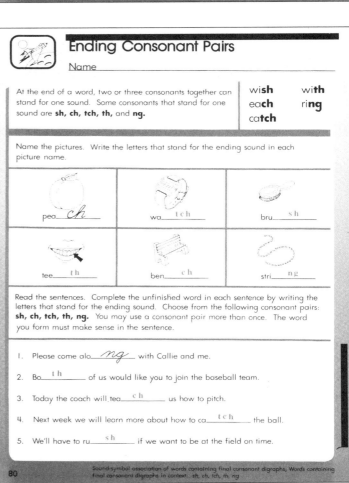

pea _ch_	wa t c h	bru s h
tee t h	ben c h	stri n g

Read the sentences. Complete the unfinished word in each sentence by writing the letters that stand for the ending sound. Choose from the following consonant pairs: **sh, ch, tch, th, ng.** You may use a consonant pair more than once. The word you form must make sense in the sentence.

1. Please come alo _ng_ with Callie and me.

2. Bo___t h___ of us would like you to join the baseball team.

3. Today the coach will tea___c h___ us how to pitch.

4. Next week we will learn more about how to ca___t c h___ the ball.

5. We'll have to ru___s h___ if we want to be at the field on time.

80   Sound-symbol association of words containing final consonant digraphs; Words containing final consonant digraphs in context. sh, ch, tch, th, ng

Page 81 — Ending Consonant Pairs

Ending Consonant Pairs

Name _____

Words to use: dish, such, catch, sang, fish, each, patch, bath, swing, peach, hatch, tooth

Read each sentence and the words beside it. Write the word that makes sense in each sentence.

1. The band will __march__ onto the field and play the school song.
   - match
   - math
   - march

2. This morning we bought enough __string__ for two kites.
   - scratch
   - splash
   - string

3. A large __branch__ was broken off our elm tree during the storm.
   - both
   - brush
   - branch

4. The picture will turn out better if you use a __flash__ on your camera.
   - flash
   - splash
   - crash

5. How many __teeth__ does the baby have now?
   - teach
   - teeth
   - leash

6. When the bell __rang__, the children hurried from the playground to the classroom.
   - ranch
   - rash
   - rang

7. Our sleds made a __path__ through the snowy woods.
   - path
   - patch
   - peach

8. The __switch__ on this lamp is broken.
   - switch
   - such
   - swing

9. The kitten didn't mean to __scratch__ you.
   - spring
   - scratch
   - sang

10. When I visit my cousins' farm, I like to __brush__ the horses.
    - branch
    - booth
    - brush

Words containing final consonant digraphs in context: sh, ch, tch, th, ng   81

Page 82 — Consonant Pairs

Consonant Pairs

Name _____

The letters **gh** sometimes stand for the sound of **f**, as in lau**gh**. The letters **ph** usually stand for the sound of **f**, as in ele**ph**ant.

lau**gh**   ele**ph**ant

Read the words and look at the pictures. Circle the word that tells about each picture.

| (photo) tough | alphabet laughing | phone (cough) |
| tough (telephone) | (laugh) photo | enough (elephant) |

Read the sentences and the word choices. Circle the word that makes sense in each sentence.

1. Will you answer the (telephone, rough) while I am reading?
2. When we drive our car over the (phone, rough) road, we bounce on the seats.
3. Sammy likes to take (laugh, photos) when he's on a trip.
4. When you visited the zoo, did you see the baby (elephant, rough)?
5. The meat is too (phone, tough) to cut with this knife.
6. Does Sandy have (enough, telephone) paper for art class?
7. Rosa makes faces to make the baby (laugh, photo).

82   Symbol-sound association of words containing consonant digraphs; Words containing consonant digraphs in context: gh, ph

Page 83 — Consonant Pairs

Consonant Pairs

Name _____

Read the list of words below. Then read the sentences that follow. Write the word from the list that makes sense in each sentence.

tough	elephant	telephone	alphabet
laugh	enough	rough	nephew
microphone	rougher	photograph	laughing

1. You may want to use a __microphone__ when you speak to large groups.
2. Will Brad have __enough__ time to visit us this week?
3. Dad is teaching Sue the letters of the __alphabet__.
4. I know you'll __laugh__ when you read this funny story.
5. Because the wood of the chair is __rough__, we'll use sandpaper to make it smooth.
6. My sister is my aunt's niece, and my brother is her __nephew__.
7. The children were __laughing__ at the circus clown.
8. I am sorry that the meat I cooked is so __tough__.
9. This road is __rougher__ than it was last winter.
10. I can't hear the __telephone__ ringing when I'm working outside.
11. Ann wants to give me a __photograph__ of her cats.
12. Val has always wanted to feed peanuts to an __elephant__.

Words containing gh and ph in context   83

Page 84 — Consonant Pairs

Consonant Pairs

Name _____

Read the list of words below. Then read the clues that follow. Write the word from the list that matches each clue.

| rough | tough | laugh | telephone | photo |
| nephew | enough | alphabet | elephant | |

1. not smooth — __rough__
2. what you do when you think something is funny — __laugh__
3. a boy who has an aunt or uncle — __nephew__
4. starts with **a, b, c** — __alphabet__
5. as much as is needed — __enough__
6. something you can use to talk with another person — __telephone__
7. hard to chew or cut — __tough__
8. a picture that is taken with a camera — __photo__
9. a large circus animal — __elephant__

Read the sentences and the word choices. Circle the word that makes sense in each sentence.

1. Her little sister knows the letters of the (alphabet, elephant).
2. Please answer the (tough, telephone) for me.
3. The bark of that tree feels very (rough, laugh).
4. I would like to see the (enough, photos) you took with your camera.
5. The jokes in your book made me (nephew, laugh).

84   Words containing gh and ph; Words containing gh and ph in context

Consonant Pairs

Name

Read each clue. Write **sh, ch, wh, ng,** or **gh** to complete the word that matches the clue.

1. a food made from milk   __ch__eese
2. something you blow into that makes a high noise   __wh__istle
3. a tool used for digging   __sh__ovel
4. two pieces of bread with meat between them   sandwi__ch__
5. a playground toy you can sit on   swi__ng__
6. hard to cut   tou__gh__
7. something you make when you jump into water   spla__sh__

Read each clue. Write **th, ph, thr,** or **tch** to complete the word that matches the clue.

1. something that can feel sore when you have a cold   __thr__oat
2. a number greater than two   __thr__ee
3. a picture taken with a camera   __ph__oto
4. a part of your hand   __th__umb
5. a piece of cloth that covers a hole in a piece of clothing   pa__tch__
6. something that is used to make clothes   clo__th__
7. something used to light a candle   ma__tch__

Review of words containing initial and final consonant digraphs   85

Consonant Pairs

Name

Read each set of sentences and its list of words. Write the word from the list that makes sense in each sentence.

1. My family likes to _watch_ parades.
2. We always go early so that we can sit on a _bench_.
3. The last parade we saw had _thirty_ marching bands.
4. I clapped as I saw each one _march_ by.
5. When I knew the tunes, I would _sing_ along.
6. I was surprised to see a float being pulled by an _elephant_.
7. If I were in a parade, the children would _laugh_ at my funny clown costume.

march
laugh
thumb
watch
elephant
bench
sing
thirty
catch

1. I _wish_ this room looked nicer.
2. I wonder if I should paint the walls _white_.
3. Should I keep _both_ the lamp and the basket on that table?
4. Shall I put two or _three_ pictures on this wall?
5. Where should I hang this _shelf_ for my books?
6. Please tell me what you _think_ about this chair.
7. Did I hear you say, "Don't _change_ a thing"?

shelf
both
wish
whisper
three
white
shake
change
think

86   Assessment of words containing initial and final consonant digraphs in context

---

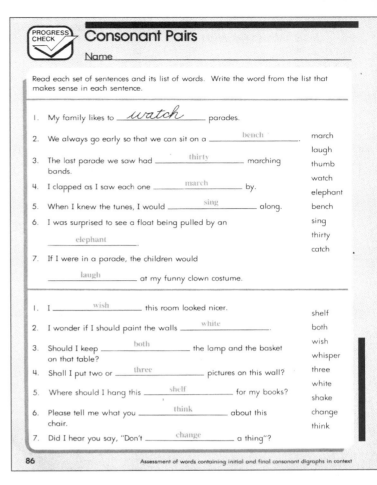

Vowels With *R*

Name

When a vowel is followed by the letter **r**, the vowel stands for a special sound that is neither long nor short. For example, **ar** stands for the sound you hear in **jar**; **er, ir,** and **ur** stand for the sounds you hear in **fern, bird,** and **burn; or** stands for the sound you hear in **horn**.

jar   horn
fern burn
bird

Name the pictures and read the sentences. Circle the word in each sentence that has the same vowel sound as the picture name.

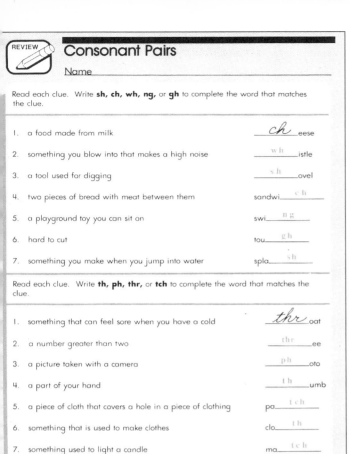

barn
1. This spring we'll be planting corn in our (garden.)

fork
2. Amy's brother is too (short) to see out the car window.

arm
3. I would like to knit a (scarf) that will match the color of this skirt.

horse
4. The kitten likes to curl up and sleep on the front (porch.)

bird
5. My friends and I put on a make-believe (circus) in the park.

jar
6. An (artist) could turn this white wall into a beautiful picture.

turtle
7. If you (turn) down this path, you will see a pine forest.

Sound-symbol association of words containing r-controlled vowels   87

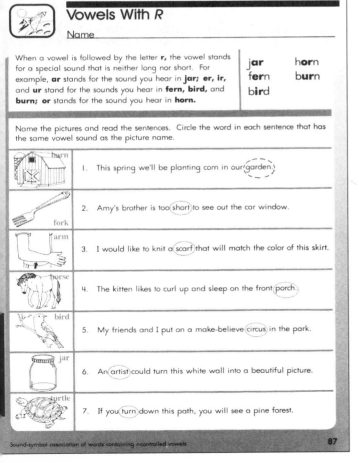

Vowels With *R*

Name

Read the list of words below. Then read the questions that follow. Write the word from the list that answers each question.

turkey	porch	nurse	storm	stars
scarf	dirt	forest	slippers	herd
purple	thirty	card	ladder	

1. What is a large bird?   _turkey_
2. In what is a seed planted?   _dirt_
3. What brings snow or rain?   _storm_
4. What can you sign and send in the mail?   _card_
5. What can be worn on your feet?   _slippers_
6. What can you wear to keep your head or neck warm?   _scarf_
7. Who helps care for people who are ill?   _nurse_
8. What can you use to climb to high places?   _ladder_
9. What has many trees?   _forest_
10. What is a group of cows called?   _herd_
11. What can be seen in the sky at night?   _stars_
12. What number comes after twenty-nine?   _thirty_
13. What is a color?   _purple_
14. What can be on the front of a house?   _porch_

88   Words containing r-controlled vowels in context

189

Read the sentences and the word choices. Circle the word that makes sense in each sentence.

1. I go to the craft center with my friends each Saturday ((morning), market).
2. The ((teachers), torch) show us a different craft every week.
3. One time, we made little ((lanterns), large) out of tin.
4. Another time, I used a new kind of paint to color a white ((shirt), sharp).
5. I have made a scarf out of yarn and a belt out of (ladder, (leather)).
6. Sometimes I make mistakes, but most of my things (torn, (turn)) out all right.
7. My work at the center makes me want to become an ((artist), other).

1. Last night's storm made a mess of our ((yard), yarn).
2. Now we must try to save the plants in our (germ, (garden)).
3. Our tall green corn plants are now lying in the ((dirt), dart).
4. I'll use a broom to sweep the front (perch, (porch)).
5. My older brother and my ((sister), squirrel) will get the tree branches off the roof.
6. We are lucky that the storm did not (her, (hurt)) the apple tree we just planted.
7. I hope the wind doesn't blow so ((hard), horn) in the next storm.

Read each sentence and look at the letter pairs beside it. Write one of the letter pairs to complete the unfinished word in each sentence. The word you form must make sense in the sentence.

1. We planted rows of seeds in the g_ar_den.   ar, er
2. I like to watch the dancer t_ur_n when he dances on the stage.   or, ur
3. The tail of the squ_ir_rel is bushy.   ar, ir
4. Before it snows, we will cov_er_ the plants in our garden.   or, er
5. A sales cl_er_k will be able to help you find a shirt in your size.   er, or
6. We put our bikes in the shed when it began to st_or_m.   ur, or
7. I feed my t_ur_tle once a day in the morning.   or, ur
8. There are seats for f_or_ty children in the classroom.   ir, or
9. We buy our eggs and milk at a f_ar_m.   or, ar
10. You'll find the answ_er_ to your question in this book.   or, er
11. Shane would like to try out for a p_ar_t in the play.   ir, ar
12. The hamm_er_ hit my thumb instead of the nail.   er, ar
13. This ch_ar_t shows how far I have run this spring.   ar, er
14. Carla has my comb in her p_ur_se.   ar, ur
15. The group must form a c_ir_cle before the game begins.   ar, ir

---

Read the sentences and the list of words. Write the word from the list that makes sense in each sentence.

1. A _turtle_ is a good pet to keep in a small home.
2. There are twelve fresh eggs in the _carton_.
3. The balloon made a loud noise when it _burst_.
4. That pile of _dirt_ must be moved before the building begins.
5. The artist uses gold and _silver_ to make bracelets.
6. My baby brother is too _short_ to reach the doorknob.
7. Which runner do you think will be the _first_ to cross the finish line?
8. Please pass the salt and _pepper_ shakers to me.
9. What kind of wood will _burn_ best in a fireplace?
10. Sometimes my dog _barks_ when I won't let her come outside with me.
11. Our class will hear a _speaker_ talk about her trip to Spain.
12. My older sister lives in an _apartment_ near our house.
13. I know spring is near when I hear the birds _chirp_.
14. The puppy was _born_ three weeks ago.

burn
first
chirp
pepper
silver
apartment
dirt
burst
speaker
born
turtle
barks
short
carton

Read the list of words below. Then read the sentences that follow. Write the word from the list that makes sense in each sentence.

porch	better	squirrels	thirty
hurry	alarm	slippers	birthday
parking	forget	horse	hurt

1. After school I come home and sit on the front _porch_.
2. I like to watch the _squirrels_ run through the trees.
3. They make me _forget_ the cares of my day.
4. Don takes lessons to learn how to ride a _horse_.
5. His teacher says that Don's riding is getting _better_ every week.
6. I'll be going to Kate's surprise _birthday_ party next week.
7. The party will be held at the park behind the school _parking_ lot.
8. I must _hurry_ to get to the post office.
9. The mail will be picked up there in _thirty_ minutes.
10. I jumped out of bed when the _alarm_ rang this morning.
11. One of my _slippers_ fell off as I ran down the hallway.
12. I'm surprised I didn't _hurt_ myself as I hurried through the house.

190

The letters **oi** and **oy** stand for the vowel sounds in **coin** and **toys.** The letters **ou** and **ow** often stand for the vowel sounds you hear in **cloud** and **cow.**

| c**oi**n | cl**ou**d |
| t**oy**s | c**ow** |

Read the list of words below. Then look at the pictures. Write a word from the list that tells about each picture.

cloud   point   frown   boy   boil   bounce

cloud

boy

point

boil

bounce

frown

Read the sentences and the word choices. Circle the word that makes sense in each sentence.

1. Last weekend my cousin and I were looking (around, allow) his basement.
2. We (foil, found) a trunk that was full of old picture books.
3. One book had a picture of a different circus (cloud, clown) on each page.
4. Another book had drawings of beautiful (flowers, found).
5. My cousin's mother told me I could have my (crowd, choice) of the old books.
6. I (join, enjoy) looking at the book about animals that I took home.

Read each sentence and the words beside it. Write the word that makes sense in each sentence.

1. My neighbor's little ___boy___ likes to ride his bicycle on the bike path. — boil / boy

2. My sister can name the different kinds of ___clouds___ in the sky. — clouds / coins

3. Every child in that family has a beautiful singing ___voice___. — voice / vow

4. The ___royal___ princess told the children a story. — royal / round

5. We learned that some plants can have ___poison___ in them. — pound / poison

6. Rose tries to see how high the basketball will ___bounce___. — boiling / bounce

7. I would like to take a picture of the sand castle before the waves ___destroy___ it. — down / destroy

8. Is this dark ___soil___ good for growing corn? — scout / soil

9. When we walked through the barn, I saw a ___mouse___ run across the floor. — mouse / mouth

10. The young girl ___frowned___ when she lost her balloon. — frowned / found

---

Read the clues and the list of words. Write the word from the list that matches each clue.

1. something that helps to keep machines running — _oil_
2. sounds — noises
3. to yell — shout
4. a large bird — owl
5. a farm tool that loosens dirt — plow
6. things that children play with — toys
7. a group of many people — crowd
8. to hit with a hammer — pound
9. something that water does when it is very hot — boils
10. dirt — soil
11. the sharp end of something — point
12. the part of the face used to smile — mouth
13. a very tall building — tower
14. a young man — boy
15. a sea animal that lives in a shell — oyster

pound
oil
shout
tower
plow
soil
noises
point
boy
toys
boils
crowd
mouth
owl
oyster

Read each sentence and look at the letter pairs beside it. Write one of the letter pairs to complete the unfinished word in each sentence. The word you form must make sense in the sentence.

1. I will see if Dad will all___ow___ me to take the bus. — ow, oi
2. I would like to ride to t___ow___n with my friend Beth. — oy, ow
3. If we go right after school, there will be no cr___ow___ds in the stores. — ow, oy
4. Beth knows how to get ar___ou___nd from one place to another. — ou, oi
5. She will help me find a t___oy___ for Timmy's birthday. — oy, ou
6. We will go to a shop that sells stamps and c___oi___ns. — ow, oi
7. Beth thinks I will enj___oy___ looking in the other store windows, too. — ou, oy
8. We are planning to return to Beth's h___ou___se before it gets dark. — oi, ou

1. Last spring I wanted to j___oi___n an outdoors club. — oi, ow
2. My friend Joy told me about being a sc___ou___t. — oi, ou
3. I would enj___oy___ being a member of the group. — oy, ou
4. Our hike up Snowball M___ou___ntain was one I'll never forget. — ou, oi
5. The hike back d___ow___n to our campsite was not easy because the mountain paths are steep. — oi, ow
6. I am pr___ou___d to be a part of the group. — ou, oi

OI, OY, OU, and OW

Name _____

Read the sentences and the word choices. Circle the word that makes sense in each sentence.

1. Flowers will grow well in this rich (sound, (soil)).
2. The singer works hard to make his ((voice), choice) sound better.
3. When I went shopping, I bought eggs, milk, and a bag of (frown, (flour)).
4. Martha and Sandra are building a tall ((tower), powder) of blocks.
5. The princess doll wears a golden (count, (crown)) on her head.
6. I like to ((bounce), bow) the ball when I am on the school playground.
7. I have learned how to check the (out, (oil)) in our family car.
8. What kind of bath ((toys), town) do babies like best?
9. When you are so far away, I can hear you only if you (shower, (shout)).
10. My dog will (ground, (growl)) if he hears a strange noise.
11. The scientist can check for ((poisons), pound) in a plant.
12. I saw an (oil, (oyster)) shell when I visited the beach.
13. An older friend taught me how to ((pound), powder) a nail into a board.
14. The beautiful horses belong to the queen and her ((royal), voice) family.
15. The white, fluffy (clown, (clouds)) look pretty in the blue sky.
16. She has lived in this ((town), toy) since she was a young girl.
17. A little gray (mouth, (mouse)) ran across the barn.
18. Put the corn into the pan after the water begins to ((boil), bow).

OI, OY, OU, and OW

Name _____

Read the list of words below. Then read the sentences that follow. Write the word from the list that makes sense in each sentence.

ouch	clown	point	pound
frowning	boil	out	towel
boys	enjoy	join	choice

1. Let me know when the water in the pan starts to ___boil___
2. I have more than one ___pound___ of green beans to cook.
3. My family will ___enjoy___ eating something from our garden.
4. Do you know why I am ___frowning___ ?
5. I just fell ___out___ of that small oak tree.
6. I am not hurt, but I did yell "___ouch___" when I landed.
7. My sister has fun when she dresses up as a ___clown___.
8. She says it's fun to make girls and ___boys___ smile.
9. Please ___point___ to the row you would like to sit in.
10. Today you can have your ___choice___ of seats.
11. Will you ___join___ me when I go to the beach to swim?
12. Don't forget your sunglasses and a ___towel___.

Endings: -ED and -ING

Words to use: call, mop, work, slip, look, color, jump, rip, help, bat, bark, clap, shop

Name _____

Many new words can be formed by adding **-ed** or **-ing** to other words. When a word ends with one vowel followed by one consonant, double the consonant before adding **-ed** or **-ing**.

walk	walk**ing**
snap	snap**ped**

Read the words and add **-ed** and **-ing** to each one. Write the new words in the blanks.

		Add **-ed**	Add **-ing**
1.	mail	mailed	mailing
2.	hop	hopped	hopping
3.	plant	planted	planting
4.	talk	talked	talking
5.	chip	chipped	chipping

Read the list of words below. Then read each sentence that follows. Add **-ed** or **-ing** to one of the list words to complete each sentence. Write the word in the blank. The word you form must make sense in the sentence.

thank	ask	bag	stop	sweep

1. Star ___asked___ me to help her with some yard work.
2. We began by ___sweeping___ the leaves into piles.
3. Then we ___bagged___ the leaves.
4. Star and I ___stopped___ when it became too dark to work.
5. Star's dad ___thanked___ me for my help.

Endings: -ED and -ING

Name _____

Many new words can be formed by adding **-ed** or **-ing** to other words. When a word ends in **e,** drop the **e** before adding **-ed** or **-ing.** When a word ends in a consonant followed by **y,** change **y** to **i** before adding **-ed.** Do not change **y** to **i** before adding **-ing** to a word that ends in **y.**

save	sav**ing**
hurry	hurr**ied**
carry	carry**ing**

Read the words and add **-ed** and **-ing** to each one. Write the new words in the blanks.

		Add **-ed**	Add **-ing**
1.	taste	tasted	tasting
2.	cry	cried	crying
3.	wave	waved	waving
4.	hope	hoped	hoping
5.	marry	married	marrying

Read the list of words below. Then read each sentence that follows. Add **-ed** or **-ing** to one of the list words to complete each sentence. Write the word in the blank. The word you form must make sense in the sentence.

shine	try	race	carry	skate

1. Yoko hit the ball and ___raced___ toward first base.
2. My friends ___tried___ to play softball in the rain.
3. The dog is ___carrying___ a stick in its mouth.
4. Have you ever ___skated___ on that frozen pond?
5. I can't see because the light is ___shining___ in my eyes.

Endings: -S and -ES
Words to use: play (plays), marry (marries), thank (thanks), run (runs), try (tries), fry (fries), fly (flies)

Name _____

Often new words can be formed by adding **-s** or **-es** to other words. To change many words, add the letter **-s.** When a word ends in a consonant followed by **y**, change the **y** to **i** and add **-es.**

laugh	laugh**s**
marry	marr**ies**

Read the words and add **-s** or **-es** to each one. Write the new words in the blanks.

1. draw _draws_
2. copy _copies_
3. study _studies_
4. sing _sings_
5. walk _walks_
6. hurry _hurries_

Read the list of words below. Then read each sentence that follows. Add **-s** or **-es** to one of the list words to complete each sentence. The word you form must make sense in the sentence.

listen   need   like   try   help   study   make

1. My friend Marcos _likes_ to keep busy.
2. Before Marcos goes to school, he _makes_ his lunch for the next day.
3. He _listens_ carefully to his teacher.
4. After school he _helps_ young children learn to swim.
5. Marcos _tries_ his best to get to all of his little sister's baseball games.
6. When he gets home, Marcos does his homework and _studies_ for his tests.
7. I think Marcos _needs_ much longer days.

Many new words can be formed by adding **-es** to other words. When a word ends in **s, ss, sh, ch,** or **x,** add **-es.**

bus	bus**es**	pitch	pitch**es**
miss	miss**es**	mix	mix**es**
fish	fish**es**		

Read the words. Underline the **s, ss, sh, ch,** or **x** if it comes at the end of a word. Then add **-es** to these words. Write the new words in the blanks.

1. coach _coaches_
2. reach _reaches_
3. push _pushes_
4. pass _passes_
5. dress _dresses_
6. wax _waxes_

Read the sentences and the list of words. Add **-es** to one of the list words to complete each sentence. Write the word in the blank. The word you form must make sense in the sentence.

1. After school each child _dresses_ in play clothes.
2. Everyone _rushes_ to Mrs. Bello's backyard.
3. The scout leader _teaches_ children about camping.
4. James _passes_ his test when he ties the knots.
5. He _wishes_ that he could spend the night at the lake.
6. Alma _brushes_ the dirt from her backpack.
7. She pitches a tent while Tony _watches_ every step.
8. Using the campfire, Lin _fixes_ a snack.

teach
dress
rush
watch
pass
fix
wish
brush

Base Words and Endings
Words to use: helped (help), doing (do), studied (study), fixes (fix), skipped (skip), chopped (chop), drying (dry), dresses (dress), stopped (stop), hoping (hope), works (work)

Name _____

A word to which an ending can be added is called a base word.

reaches

Read each word and write its base word in the blank.

1. closing _close_
2. knowing _know_
3. skipped _skip_
4. batting _bat_
5. standing _stand_
6. makes _make_
7. dried _dry_
8. skating _skate_
9. stepped _step_
10. misses _miss_
11. tasted _taste_
12. copies _copy_

Read the list of base words below. Then read each sentence that follows. Complete the sentence by adding the ending shown beside the sentence to a word from the list. Write the new word in the blank.

bake   talk   try   run   find   fish

1. One day we were _talking_ about ways that we have fun. -ing
2. Andrew told us he _fishes_ in a pond near his home. -es
3. Molly said she _finds_ seashells on the beach. -s
4. Jim _tried_ to explain a guessing game he likes. -ed
5. Allen said he likes _running_ in a race more than anything else. -ing
6. Jessie told how she had a lot of fun when she _baked_ bread for her friends. -ed

---

In many words, the ending **-er** means "more." It can be used to compare two things. The ending **-est** means "most." It can be used to compare three or more things.

deep	deep**er**
deep	deep**est**

Read the sentences and the word choices. Circle the word that makes sense in each sentence.

1. This year's dog show should be (greater, greatest) than last year's show.
2. There will be a race to see which of the many dogs can run (faster, fastest).
3. Seth hopes that his dog is (quicker, quickest) than his cousin's dog.
4. A prize will be given to the (smaller, smallest) of all the dogs.
5. The (younger, youngest) dog of all might be one of Spot's puppies.
6. My dog may be the (older, oldest) dog there, but she is also the best dog in the show!

Read each sentence and the word beside it. Add **-er** or **-est** to the word to complete the sentence. Write the new word in the blank. The word you form must make sense in the sentence.

1. I must be the _slowest_ shopper in this town. slow
2. To save money, I try to find the _lowest_ of all the prices. low
3. Because I am _taller_ than I was last year, I must buy some new clothes. tall
4. My dad says I might have to buy the _highest_ priced pants in the store. high
5. I guess I take a _longer_ time choosing my things than you do. long

Endings: -ER and -EST

Name

Many new words can be formed by adding **-er** or **-est** to other words. When a word ends with one vowel followed by one consonant, double the consonant before adding **-er** or **-est**. When a word ends in **e**, drop the **e** before adding **-er** or **-est**. When a word ends in a consonant followed by **y**, change the **y** to **i** before adding **-er** or **-est**.

wet	wet**test**
wise	wis**er**
cloudy	cloud**ier**

Add **-er** and **-est** to each word below. Write the new words in the blanks.

		Add **-er**	Add **-est**
1.	busy	busier	busiest
2.	big	bigger	biggest
3.	sunny	sunnier	sunniest
4.	late	later	latest
5.	light	lighter	lightest

Read each sentence and the word beside it. Add **-er** or **-est** to the word to complete the sentence. Write the new word in the blank. The word you form must make sense in the sentence.

1. Lance's shop has the _cutest_ stuffed toys I've seen.   cute
2. The orange cat is _fatter_ than my yellow cat.   fat
3. That clown has the _funniest_ hat that I've seen.   funny
4. You'd like seeing the deer that is _taller_ than a person.   tall
5. The shop has the _finest_ toys of any store in town.   fine

Endings: -ER and -EST

Name

Read each sentence and the word shown below the blank. Add **-er** or **-est** to the word to complete the sentence. Write the new word in the blank.

1. This book is _sillier_ than the book about the pink turtle.
   (silly)
2. Will the stove get _hotter_ than it is now?
   (hot)
3. Can you make this room look _neater_ than it looked before?
   (neat)
4. Please buy the _brightest_ poster you can find.
   (bright)
5. Is that the _biggest_ of all the hot-air balloons in the show?
   (big)
6. Where can I buy the _nicest_ flowers in town?
   (nice)
7. The day of the school play is our _busiest_ day of the year.
   (busy)
8. This metal ring is _looser_ than the wooden ring I used to have.
   (loose)
9. Ellen's apartment is _closer_ to the school than mine is.
   (close)
10. The baby looked _happier_ after she took her nap.
   (happy)
11. Brenda's dog is _fatter_ than Ken's dog.
   (fat)

REVIEW   Endings

Name

Read the list of words below. Then read each sentence that follows. Complete the sentence by adding one of the endings shown beside the sentence to a word from the list. Write the new word in the blank. The word you form must make sense in the sentence.

| fish | bat | chase | study | jump | bake |

1. Tim's father _bakes_ bread in the new oven.   -s, -es
2. Peggy _fishes_ for trout in a stream near the park.   -s, -es
3. Will you be _batting_ in the next baseball game?   -ed, -ing
4. Len _studies_ his spelling words each morning.   -es, -ing
5. Elena _jumped_ into the swimming pool from the diving board.   -ed, -ing
6. Today I _chased_ my kitten around the house.   -ed, -ing

Add **-er** and **-est** to each word below. Write the new words in the blanks.

		Add **-er**	Add **-est**
1.	slow	slower	slowest
2.	sad	sadder	saddest
3.	fine	finer	finest
4.	pretty	prettier	prettiest
5.	large	larger	largest
6.	loud	louder	loudest

Plurals: -S and -ES

Name

A word that stands for one of something is a singular word. A word that stands for two or more of something is a plural word. To write the plural form of most words, add **-s**. To form the plural of a word that ends in **s**, **ss**, **sh**, **ch**, or **x**, add **-es**. To form the plural of a word that ends in a consonant followed by **y**, change the **y** to **i** and add **-es**.

toy	toy**s**
lunch	lunch**es**
baby	bab**ies**

Read the words. Write the plural form of each one.

1.	shoe	shoes	5.	boss	bosses
2.	watch	watches	6.	room	rooms
3.	brush	brushes	7.	puppy	puppies
4.	party	parties	8.	fox	foxes

Read the sentences and the list of words. Write the plural form of a word from the list to complete each sentence. The word you form must make sense in the sentence.

1. We can ride our _bikes_ to the market.   row
2. Let's go after we eat and do the _dishes_.   box
3. Eva wants us to buy some _daisies_ that can be planted.   dish
4. She will plant them in the ground in straight _rows_.   six
   bike
5. We can pay for the flowers with five dollars and some _pennies_.   penny
   daisy
6. We will ask for _boxes_ to hold the daisies we buy.   story

Plurals: Changing *F* to *V*

Words to use: elf, life, wife, loaf, knife, calf, half

Name

To write the plural form of most words that end in **f** or **fe**, change the **f** or **fe** to **v** and add **-es**.	leaf	lea**ves**
	life	li**ves**

Read each sentence and the words beside it. Write the plural form of one of the words to complete each sentence. The word you form must make sense in the sentence.

1. The cook uses sharp _knives_ to cut the meat.
   life / knife

2. How many _loaves_ of bread are needed to make forty sandwiches?
   loaf / leaf

3. In this make-believe story, a group of _elves_ makes a family very happy.
   shelf / elf

4. Most of those _calves_ were born last week.
   calf / half

5. The tree grows new _leaves_ each spring.
   leaf / life

6. This book tells about the _lives_ of well-known men and women.
   life / loaf

7. In the play, a bank was robbed by two _thieves_.
   thief / knife

8. My brother and sister learned how to build _shelves_ for their books.
   shelf / self

Forming plurals of nouns ending in f and fe
109

Irregular Plurals

Words to use: man, tooth, child, mouse, woman, goose, foot, sheep

Name

The plurals of some words are formed by changing the spelling of their singular forms.

child - children	man - men	woman - women
tooth - teeth	foot - feet	mouse - mice
goose - geese		

The plural forms of some words can be the same as their singular forms.

| sheep | deer | fish |

Read each set of sentences and its list of words. Write the plural form of a word from the list to complete each sentence. The word you form must make sense in the sentence.

1. _Children_ will enjoy seeing the puppet show.
   man / fish / Child / foot / goose / sheep / mouse

2. How much wool can you get from six _sheep_?

3. I have seen _geese_ flying over our campsite.

4. Many women and _men_ will vote tomorrow.

5. I found a nest of baby _mice_ that were each smaller than my thumb.

1. Every morning, Dad asks me if I have brushed my _teeth_.
   fish / woman / deer / tooth / child / foot / mouse

2. We need more men and _women_ to drive the school buses.

3. If we wait near the woods, we might see some _deer_ (deers is also acceptable).

4. The new shoes I am wearing make my _feet_ hurt.

5. Joy came home carrying a pail filled with _fish_ (fishes is also acceptable) that she caught at the lake.

110   Forming irregular plurals in context

Plurals

Words to use: key, song, bench, boss, elf, life, glove, brush, wife, candle, lunch, loaf, dollar, jelly, knife, neighbor, bunny, fish, mountain, puppy, sheep, fox, party, goose

Name

Read the paragraphs and the list of words. Write the plural form of a word from the list to complete each sentence. The words you form must make sense in the paragraph.

I think you will like this store better than the _stores_ we shopped in before. It is full of things for _children_ under the age of twelve. The clothing part of the store has jeans, shirts, and _dresses_. Another part of the store has _watches_ to tell time, as well as rings and bracelets.

Most children like to look at the toys. They are in the biggest part of the store. The _shelves_ are full of every kind of toy. There are dolls that look like newborn _babies_, and dolls that are dressed like grown men and _women_. I have seen sets of _dishes_ you could eat from and small sinks and stoves. There are also toy foods, such as apples and _peaches_.

You might like seeing the stuffed animals like those puppies and _calves_. I never leave the store without looking at the _games_ that can be played by one or more players. You can see why I save my _pennies_ before I visit this store!

watch / baby / calf / store / peach / shelf / dress / dish / penny / child / game / woman

Forming plurals in context
111

Showing Ownership

Name

To make most words show ownership, add an apostrophe (') and **s**. In the example, **dog's bone**, the **'s** shows that the bone belongs to the dog.	dog**'s** bone

Rewrite each group of words below, adding **'s** to form words that show ownership.

1. the horse that Bruce owns — _Bruce's horse_
2. the sock that the baby wears — _baby's sock_
3. the windows of a truck — _truck's windows_
4. the backpack that Sal owns — _Sal's backpack_
5. the game that belongs to Kim — _Kim's game_
6. the paw of a cat — _cat's paw_

Read each sentence and the words beside it. Add **'s** to one of the words to complete the sentence. The word you form must make sense in the sentence.

1. The _bank's_ doors open each day at nine o'clock.
   bank / book

2. My _aunt's_ office is in the center of the town.
   apple / aunt

3. Her _father's_ speech was heard by many people.
   father / farm

4. The _bush's_ flowers are light pink.
   brush / bush

5. My math _teacher's_ writing is easy to read.
   teacher / tractor

112   Forming singular possessives in isolation and in context

195

Showing Ownership

Name _____

To make a singular word show ownership, add an apostrophe (') and **s**. To make a plural word that ends in **s** show ownership, add just an apostrophe. In the examples, **'s** shows that the bones belong to one dog, and **s'** shows that the bones belong to more than one dog.

dog**'s** bones
dogs**'** bones

Read the words and look at the pictures. Circle the words that tell about each picture.

girl's gloves (girls' gloves)	tree's bark trees' bark	truck's wheels trucks' wheels
dog's food (dogs' food)	boy's photos boys' photos	skunk's stripes (skunks' stripes)

Rewrite each group of words below, adding ' or 's to the underlined word to show ownership.

1. the wings of the <u>birds</u> — *birds' wings*

2. the tent that is used by the <u>scouts</u> — scouts' tent

3. the house that belongs to a <u>teacher</u> — teacher's house

4. the office used by two <u>dentists</u> — dentists' office

5. the covers of the <u>books</u> — books' covers

6. the tail of a <u>monkey</u> — monkey's tail

Showing Ownership

Name _____

Read each sentence and the words shown below the blank. Write the word that makes sense in the sentence.

1. The ____*dog's*____ tail is short and brown.
   (dog's, dogs')

2. The two ____trucks'____ steering wheels are the same color.
   (truck's, trucks')

3. That ____flag's____ stripes are green and white.
   (flag's, flags')

4. The ____boys'____ birthdays are on the same day.
   (boy's, boys')

5. Did you see ____Mary's____ new puppy?
   (Marys', Mary's)

6. I could see the ____cats'____ heads through the little window.
   (cat's, cats')

7. My youngest ____sister's____ blocks are on her bedroom floor.
   (sister's, sisters')

8. We found ____Mother's____ hammer under the steps.
   (Mother's, Mothers')

9. The ____kitten's____ coat is always kept clean.
   (kittens', kitten's)

10. The ____rooms'____ floors are made of wood.
    (room's, rooms')

11. My ____friend's____ nose was sunburned yesterday.
    (friend's, friends')

12. The ____cars'____ engines were made in this city.
    (car's, cars')

Plurals and Showing Ownership

Name _____

Read the words and write the plural form of each one.

1. bicycle — *bicycles*
2. wolf — wolves
3. school — schools
4. baby — babies
5. child — children
6. box — boxes
7. apple — apples
8. party — parties
9. glass — glasses
10. man — men
11. patch — patches
12. deer — deer (deers is also acceptable)
13. elf — elves
14. puppy — puppies

Rewrite each group of words below, adding ' or 's to the underlined word to show ownership.

1. the whiskers of the <u>cats</u> — *cats' whiskers*

2. the field that is used by the <u>players</u> — players' field

3. the apartment that belongs to <u>Joan</u> — Joan's apartment

4. the library used by the <u>teachers</u> — teachers' library

5. the playground owned by the <u>school</u> — school's playground

6. the hats worn by the <u>fire fighters</u> — fire fighters' hats

7. the smile of the <u>child</u> — child's smile

8. the backpack that belongs to <u>Bob</u> — Bob's backpack

Endings and Plurals

Name _____

Read each sentence and the word beside it. Complete each sentence by adding one of the endings shown below to the word. Write the new word in the blank. The word you form must make sense in the sentence.

-ed	-ing	-s	-es	-er	-est

1. A storm began while we were *playing* in the yard.   play

2. That is the ____silliest____ hat I have ever seen!   silly

3. A few of us ____carried____ the logs for the fire.   carry

4. Aunt Janet ____thanks____ me every time I visit.   thank

5. When Dave's football clothes are dirty, he _____ them.   wash

6. The crowd ____clapped____ when the show was over.   clap

7. Celina seems ____happier____ today than she was yesterday.   happy

8. Every afternoon a jet ____flies____ over our house.   fly

Read the words and write the plural form of each one.

1. brush — *brushes*
2. friend — friends
3. box — boxes
4. book — books
5. buggy — buggies
6. knife — knives
7. mouse — mice
8. city — cities
9. match — matches
10. shelf — shelves
11. sheep — sheep
12. class — classes

Pick Up Page 116 From Teacher Annotated Edition at 45%

Showing Ownership

Name _____

Read each sentence and the words beside it. Write the word that makes sense in each sentence.

1. This spelling _____book's_____ pages are ripped.
   - book's
   - books'

2. Her _____brothers'_____ bedrooms are painted red and blue.
   - brother's
   - brothers'

3. Our many _____trees'_____ leaves are different shades of green.
   - tree's
   - trees'

4. _____Jack's_____ school was built last year.
   - Jack's
   - Jacks'

5. The three _____clowns'_____ noses were shiny and red.
   - clown's
   - clowns'

6. The bedroom _____phone's_____ ring woke me up.
   - phone's
   - phones'

7. The _____park's_____ lawn is always green.
   - park's
   - parks'

8. All of these _____pictures'_____ frames are made of wood and metal.
   - picture's
   - pictures'

9. The _____elephants'_____ trunks are strong enough to carry logs.
   - elephant's
   - elephants'

10. My oldest _____sister's_____ shoe size is a five.
   - sister's
   - sisters'

Assessment of using singular and plural possessives in context 117

Reading and Writing Wrap-Up

Name _____

The Boy Who Cried "Wolf!"

This is a story that teaches something important about life. Read to see if you can find out what it is.

Once there was a boy who looked after sheep. He had nothing to do all day but watch the sheep, and he was bored.

One day the boy thought of a way to have some fun, so he ran into the village shouting, "Wolf! Wolf! A wolf is after the sheep!"

All the people in the village left their work to help the boy. But when they reached the place where the sheep were grazing, there was no wolf in sight. The boy laughed at the people for believing his trick. The next day the boy played the same trick. Now he was having fun.

On the third day, the boy saw a hungry wolf coming near the flock, and he got very frightened. He ran as fast as his legs would carry him to the village. "Help!" he cried. "A wolf is going to kill the sheep!"

But this time the people did not leave their work to help the boy. They said, "That boy is just trying to fool us again by telling another lie." When the boy returned to the sheep, he saw that the wolf had killed them all.

The people were very angry when they found out the boy had not been telling a lie this time. They said, "People who tell lies cannot be believed even when they say something that is true."

A. Answer the following questions.
1. What was the job of the boy in the story?
   The boy was a shepherd or sheep herder. He took care of sheep.

2. Why did the boy play a trick?
   He was bored. He wanted to have some fun.

3. What did the people do the first time the boy played his trick?
   They ran to help him.

118 Application of reading and comprehension skills in a literature context

---

Literature

Name _____

B. Check the two words in each line that have the same meaning in the story.

1. _____ play   ✔ fool   ✔ trick
2. ✔ flock   ✔ sheep   _____ grazing

C. Answer the following questions.
1. What does this story teach about life?
   The story teaches that if you tell lies, no one will believe you even when
   you tell the truth.

2. Do you think the people were right or wrong not to believe the boy the third time he cried, "Wolf"? Tell why or why not.
   Answers will vary.

D. Write a story about one of the following sayings.

If you want something to be done right, do it yourself.
In time of trouble, you find out who your true friends are.
Those who harm others often end up harming themselves.

Answer will vary.

_____
_____
_____
_____

Application of thinking and writing skills in a literature context 119

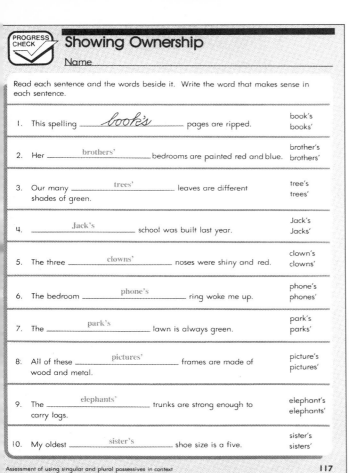

Compound Words

Words to use: wishbone, highway, rainbow, snowstorm, blueberry, lifeboat, playhouse, baseball, airport, footprint, runway

Name _____

A compound word is formed by joining two smaller words together.

dog + house = doghouse

Read each compound word and write the two words that form it.

1. waterfall   water   fall
2. snowflakes   snow   flakes
3. grandson   grand   son
4. bookcase   book   case
5. doorbell   door   bell
6. rainstorm   rain   storm
7. lighthouse   light   house

Read the sentences. Circle the two compound words in each sentence.

1. Can you use your (snowplow) on our (driveway)?
2. I found a (starfish) and a few (seashells) on the beach.
3. Jean will fold the (bedspread) that goes in her (bedroom).
4. My (grandfather) makes (homemade) bean soup.
5. I must have left my (raincoat) on the (playground).
6. Have you ever watched a (sunset) from the tall building (downtown)?
7. The plants will not grow (without) (sunshine).

120 Identifying words that form compound words; Identifying compound words in context

Compound Words

Name _____

Words to use: lighthouse, snowplow, bookcase, raincoat, rowboat, snowflake, mailbox

Read the words in each list below. Draw lines to match the words that form compound words.

book	place	side	noon
rain	fall	snow	paper
pan	day	after	walk
fire	case	fire	storm
birth	cakes	news	wood

Read the list of words below. Then read the sentences that follow. Write the word from the list that makes sense in each sentence.

notebook	cookbook	sometimes	something	oatmeal
airplane	rowboat	grandmother	airport	

1. I plan to write to my *grandmother*, who lives in New York.

2. She will enjoy reading about my ____ rowboat ____ ride on the lake.

3. She may remember the time we went to the city ____ airport ____.

4. We flew in an ____ airplane ____ that took us over the town.

5. We did that because Grandmother wanted me to try ____ something ____ new.

6. She ____ sometimes ____ wants me to taste something I've never eaten before.

7. Once she tried to make me eat ____ oatmeal ____.

8. As a joke, I bought her a new ____ cookbook ____ to read.

9. I could fill a ____ notebook ____ with stories about Grandmother and me!

Compound Words

Name _____

Words to use: fireplace, birthday, snowball, sunshine, playground, driveway, homemade

Read the sentences below. Use two words from each sentence to form a compound word. Write the compound word in the blank.

1. A bird that is blue is called a *bluebird*

2. A walk near the side of a road is a ____ sidewalk ____

3. A cloth that covers a table is a ____ tablecloth ____

4. The bud of a rose is a ____ rosebud ____

5. A ball that is thrown through a basket is a ____ basketball ____

6. A brush that is used to clean each tooth is a ____ toothbrush ____

7. Work that is done for school is called ____ schoolwork ____

8. A shell that can be found near the sea is a ____ seashell ____

9. Corn that you can pop is called ____ popcorn ____

10. A bell that is near the door of a house is a ____ doorbell ____

11. A pot that holds tea is a ____ teapot ____

12. Wood that is used to build a fire is called ____ firewood ____

13. The print of a foot made in sand is called a ____ footprint ____

14. Work done at home is ____ homework ____

15. A tub for a bath is a ____ bathtub ____

16. A boat that has a sail is a ____ sailboat ____

Contractions

Name _____

Words to use: we will (we'll), you would (you'd), are not (aren't), should not (shouldn't), I will (I'll), he is (he's), we are (we're), they have (they've), is not (isn't)

A contraction is a short way to write two words. It is written by putting two words together and leaving out a letter or letters. An apostrophe (') takes the place of the letters that are left out. The word **won't** is a special contraction made from the words **will** and **not**.

is + not =	**isn't**
will + not =	**won't**
we + are =	**we're**
I + will =	**I'll**

Read the list of contractions below. Then read the pairs of words that follow. Write a contraction from the list that stands for each word pair.

it's	she'll	weren't
we'd	hadn't	they're

1. had not   *hadn't*

2. were not   weren't

3. they are   they're

4. she will   she'll

5. we would   we'd

6. it is   it's

Read each sentence and the pair of words shown below the blank. Complete the sentence by writing the contraction that stands for the word pair.

1. Does he know that ____ *we're* ____ coming home early?
(we are)

2. Tammy ____ couldn't ____ find the letter she wrote.
(could not)

3. John ____ wasn't ____ ready to swim in the deep end of the pool.
(was not)

4. We ____ don't ____ go to school in the summer.
(do not)

5. Did you know that ____ they've ____ been visiting their friends?
(they have)

6. Ellen ____ won't ____ be able to come to our party.
(will not)

Contractions

Name _____

Words to use: I'd, they've, here's, there's, haven't, hadn't

Read the contractions below. Then write the two words for which each contraction stands.

1. wouldn't   *would not*
2. we've   we have
3. didn't   did not
4. that's   that is or that has
5. we'd   we would or we had

6. he'll   he will
7. hasn't   has not
8. she's   she is or she has
9. won't   will not
10. I've   I have

Read each sentence and the contraction shown below the blank. Complete the sentence by writing the two words for which the contraction stands.

1. *I would* like to move to a warmer part of the country.
(I'd)

2. It ____ does not ____ snow where you live, does it?
(doesn't)

3. ____ You have ____ not seen a snowflake since you moved there.
(You've)

4. I ____ would not ____ be able to go sled riding if I lived where you live.
(wouldn't)

5. ____ It is ____ not cold enough to go ice skating, either.
(It's)

6. ____ I am ____ not sure I want to move after all.
(I'm)

Contractions

Name _____

Words to use: does not (doesn't), would not (wouldn't), will not (won't), they are (they're)

Read each sentence and find the two words in it that can be made into a contraction. Circle the two words and write the contraction in the blank.

1. The city zoo (was not) far from our school building.

   wasn't

2. It (did not) take the bus driver long to get there.

   didn't

3. Kelly and Ross (could not) wait to see the animals.

   couldn't

4. (They had) been counting the days until the trip.

   They'd

5. Kelly says that (she is) going to work in a zoo someday.

   she's

Read the sentences and the list of contractions. Write the contraction that makes sense in each sentence. The word you write must make sense in the sentence.

1. *Shouldn't* Amy read the story to the class?

2. Jordan and Juan ___weren't___ here when she read it before.

3. I think ___they'll___ be sorry they missed the funny ending.

4. I told Ms. Mendes that we ___should've___ made the story into a play.

5. She told us ___that's___ what had been planned.

6. We can start planning after ___we've___ heard the story.

they'll
that's
won't
didn't
Shouldn't
we've
weren't
should've

Forming contractions in context; Using contractions in context   125

REVIEW

Compound Words and Contractions

Name _____

Read the clues below. Use two words from each clue to form a compound word. Write the compound word in the blank.

1. a coat worn in the rain — *raincoat*
2. a boat that you can row — rowboat
3. a tie that is worn around the neck — necktie
4. work done around the house — housework
5. a book that tells you how to cook — cookbook
6. water from a stream that falls over a high place — waterfall(s)
7. a bell that is rung at the door of a home — doorbell

Read the word pairs below. Then write the contraction that stands for each word pair.

1. we are — *we're*
2. will not — won't
3. he will — he'll
4. you would — you'd
5. are not — aren't
6. they are — they're
7. we have — we've
8. have not — haven't
9. they have — they've
10. can not — can't
11. I am — I'm
12. she had — she'd
13. do not — don't
14. there is — there's

126   *Review of forming compound words; Forming contractions*

PROGRESS CHECK

Compound Words and Contractions

Name _____

Read the list of words below. Then read the sentences that follow. Choose a word from the list to complete the compound word in each sentence. The compound word you form must make sense in the sentence.

place   port   work
case   way   room

1. I read my book and finished my home*work*
2. Each of my books is now in the book case.
3. I took my bath and cleaned the tub in the bath room.
4. I helped my mom build a fire in the fire place.
5. Soon, Dad will bring my uncle home from the air port.
6. I can't wait until I see them pull into the drive way.

Read each sentence and the pair of words beside it. Complete each sentence with a contraction that stands for the word pair.

1. *I'll* show you how to make paper airplanes.   I will
2. They're not as hard to make as you may think.   They are
3. Where's the pattern for the plane you want to make?   Where is
4. I think you'd enjoy using this colored paper.   you would
5. We haven't tried folding the heavier white paper.   have not
6. Shouldn't we start with the smallest plane?   Should not

Assessment of forming compound words and contractions in context   127

Prefixes: *UN-* and *DIS-*

Name _____

Words to use: wrap (unwrap), opened (unopened), agree (disagree), appear (disappear), kind (unkind), dress (undress), fair (unfair), lucky (unlucky), cover (discover, uncover)

A prefix is a letter or group of letters that can be added to the beginning of a word. The prefixes **un-** and **dis-** mean "not" or "the opposite of." For example, the word **unlock** means "the opposite of lock." The word **dislike** means "not like."

un + lock = **un**lock
dis + like = **dis**like

Read the list of words below. Then read each sentence that follows. Add **un-** to one of the list words to complete each sentence. Write the new word in the blank. The word you form must make sense in the sentence.

safe   load   happy   lock

1. We need help to *unload* the logs from the truck.
2. The busy street is ___unsafe___ for the children who walk to school.
3. The small child looked ___unhappy___ when she let go of her balloon.
4. You will need a key to ___unlock___ the front door.

Read the list of words below. Then read each sentence that follows. Add **dis-** to one of the list words to complete each sentence. Write the new word in the blank. The word you form must make sense in the sentence.

cover   connect   agree   liked   color

1. The bright light of the sun may *discolor* the camper's tent.
2. The scientists hope to ___discover___ a cure for the illness.
3. Joey ___disliked___ singing in the class play.
4. Ms. Miller will ___disconnect___ the wire before she fixes the lamp.
5. Because we ___disagree___, we should talk about the problem.

128   *Forming words with prefixes un- and dis-; Words containing prefixes in context*

199

Prefixes: *RE-* and *PRE-*

Name _____

Words to use: refill, preheat, retell, prepay, replace, preschool, repaid, pregame

The prefix **re-** means "again." For example, the word **refill** means "fill again." The prefix **pre-** means "before." The word **prepay** means "pay before."

re + fill = **re**fill
pre + pay = **pre**pay

Read the clues. Add **re-** or **pre-** to the underlined base word to form a word that matches the clue.

1. to <u>wrap</u> again *rewrap*
2. to <u>test</u> before pretest
3. to <u>write</u> again rewrite
4. to <u>paint</u> again repaint
5. to <u>use</u> again reuse
6. before a <u>game</u> pregame

Read each sentence and the words beside it. Write the word that makes sense in each sentence.

1. Ardis brought a book home from her *preschool* class.
   retell / preschool / pregame

2. Do you know how to _____ replace _____ the part on the bike?
   reread / replay / replace

3. The bill was _____ prepaid _____ a week ago.
   prepaid / pregame / replayed

4. We watched the band march in the _____ pregame _____ show.
   retell / prepaid / pregame

5. Are you able to _____ retell _____ the tale you heard last night?
   reread / retell / preheat

6. Please _____ reread _____ the story for the class.
   replace / replay / reread

Prefixes: *OVER-* and *MIS-*

Name _____

Words to use: understand (misunderstand), judge (misjudge), bake (overbake), pay (overpay), place (misplace), lead (mislead), do (overdo), sleep (oversleep), eat (overeat)

The prefix **over-** means "too much." For example, the word **overdo** means "to do too much." The prefix **mis-** means "badly" or "wrongly." For example, the word **misuse** means "to use wrongly."

over + do = **over**do
mis + use = **mis**use

Read the list of words below. Then read each sentence that follows. Add **over-** to one of the list words to complete each sentence. Write the new word in the blank. The word you form must make sense in the sentence.

eat   sleep   cook   load   flow

1. Did you _____ *oversleep* _____ on the first day of school?
2. Be careful not to _____ overload _____ your book bag.
3. The rain made the river _____ overflow _____.
4. The good food made me want to _____ overeat _____.
5. If you _____ overcook _____ the meat, it will be dry.

Read the list of words below. Then read each sentence that follows. Add **mis-** to one of the list words to complete each sentence. Write the new word in the blank. The word you form must make sense in the sentence.

understand   spell   place   treat   lead

1. If you _____ *mistreat* _____ your bike, it will not run well.
2. When you _____ misspell _____ a word, cross it out and write it correctly.
3. Did you _____ misunderstand _____ what needed to be done?
4. If you _____ misplace _____ your homework, you must find it or redo it.
5. That sign will _____ mislead _____ travelers.

Prefixes

Name _____

Words to use: unlock, dislike, repaint, unload, discolor, repaid, overcrowd, mistreat, misspell, overflow, unwrap, distrust, preschool, unpack, rewrap, pregame, misprint

Read each sentence and the word beside it. Add **un-, pre-,** or **over-** to the word to complete each sentence. Write the new word in the blank. The word you form must make sense in the sentence.

1. The _____ *unfair* _____ rules were changed.   fair
2. I _____ prepaid _____ the cost at the time I ordered.   paid
3. If you don't wake her, she will _____ oversleep _____.   sleep
4. My dog _____ overeats _____ when there is too much food in the dish.   eats
5. Because I lost the game, I felt _____ unlucky _____.   lucky
6. Scott talks about his _____ preschool _____ class.   school

Read each sentence and the word beside it. Add **dis-, re-,** or **mis-** to the word to complete each sentence. Write the new word in the blank. The word you form must make sense in the sentence.

1. If you _____ *disagree* _____ with me, let me know.   agree
2. Grandma will _____ retell _____ many of her stories.   tell
3. I often _____ misjudge _____ the time when I get busy.   judge
4. I will _____ reheat _____ the chicken soup for lunch.   heat
5. We saw the rabbit _____ disappear _____ from sight into the red hat.   appear
6. If you _____ misread _____ the sign, you will get lost.   read

---

Suffixes: *-FUL* and *-LESS*

Name _____

Words to use: thought (thoughtful, thoughtless), spoon (spoonful), thank (thankful, thankless), help (helpful, helpless), cloud (cloudless), pain (painful, painless)

A suffix is a letter or group of letters that can be added to the end of a word. The suffix **-ful** usually means "full of." For example, the word **helpful** means "full of help." The suffix **-less** usually means "without." The word **hopeless** means "without hope."

help + **ful** = help**ful**
hope + **less** = hope**less**

Read the words below. Form new words by adding the suffix **-ful** or **-less** to the words. Write each word under the correct heading.

end   hand   wonder   friend   play   cloud   forget   home

Order of words may vary.

Add **-ful**	Add **-less**
handful	endless
wonderful	friendless
playful	cloudless
forgetful	homeless

Read the sentences and the list of words. Write the word from the list that makes sense in each sentence.

1. I was _____ *careless* _____ when I lost my math paper.
2. Put a small _____ spoonful _____ of salt into the soup.
3. I slept well and had a _____ restful _____ night.
4. We are _____ thankful _____ that we have friends like you.
5. I am glad the snake we saw is _____ harmless _____.
6. The list of jobs to do at home seems _____ endless _____.

careless
restful
helpful
harmless
sleepless
thankful
spoonful
endless

Suffixes: -Y and -LY

Name _____

Words to use: thirsty, loudly, bumpy, quickly, nicely, dusty, sleepy, rusty, rocky, slowly

The suffixes **-y** and **-ly** can be added to some words. For example, a day with **rain** is a **rainy** day. Something done in a **nice** way is done **nicely**.

rain + **y** = rain**y**
nice + **ly** = nice**ly**

Read the list of words below. Then read each sentence that follows. Add **-y** to one of the list words to complete each sentence. Write the new word in the blank. The word you form must make sense in the sentence.

frost   cloud   stick   luck   squeak

1. We were _**lucky**_ to get five tickets for the early show last Saturday.

2. I spilled some glue, and my desk is now _**sticky**_.

3. We didn't see much sunshine because the sky was _**cloudy**_.

4. My new boots make a _**squeaky**_ sound when I walk.

5. Because it is cold outdoors, our windows look white and _**frosty**_.

Read the list of words below. Then read each sentence that follows. Add **-ly** to one of the list words to complete each sentence. Write the new word in the blank. The word you form must make sense in the sentence.

soft   week   quick   friend   slow

1. Because he walked _**slowly**_, he missed the bus.

2. If we get dressed _**quickly**_, we can go sled riding before we eat.

3. My older brother reads a _**weekly**_ newspaper.

4. She played the song so _**softly**_ that we could hardly hear it.

5. We had fun at the party because we met some _**friendly**_ people.

Forming words with suffixes -y and -ly; Words containing suffixes in context   133

Suffixes: -ABLE and -ISH

Name _____

Words to use: reach (reachable), read (readable), child (childish), boy (boyish), girl (girlish), enjoy (enjoyable), wash (washable), baby (babyish)

The suffix **-able** means "can be" or "able to be." For example, the word **washable** means "can be washed." The suffix **-ish** means "like" or "somewhat." The word **childish** means "like a child."

wash + **able** = wash**able**
child + **ish** = child**ish**

Read the words below. Form new words by adding the suffix **-able** or **-ish** to the words. Write each word under the correct heading.

yellow   baby   break   pass   girl   like   clown   change

Add **-able**	Add **-ish**
breakable	yellowish
passable	babyish
likeable	girlish
changeable	clownish

Read the sentences and the list of words. Add **-able** or **-ish** to one of the list words to complete each sentence. Write the word in the blank. The word you form must make sense in the sentence.

1. The low shelf makes the toys _**reachable**_.

2. The pond's water looks _**greenish**_.

3. It is _**foolish**_ to cross the street without looking both ways.

4. That page got wet, so the words are no longer _**readable**_.

5. You can get the stain out of a _**washable**_ shirt.

wash
green
reach
fool
read

134   Forming words with suffixes -able and -ish; Words containing suffixes in context

---

Suffixes

Name _____

Words to use: cheerful, thankful, hopeless, thoughtless, squeaky, frosty, friendly, weekly

Read each sentence and the suffixes beside it. Add one of the suffixes to the word shown below the blank to complete the sentence. The word you form must make sense in the sentence.

1. Please speak _**loudly**_ when you give your speech.
   (loud)   -ful -ly

2. Berta has brown eyes and long, _**curly**_ brown hair.
   (curl)   -y -ful

3. After looking for my bike for an hour, I felt _**hopeless**_.
   (hope)   -less -ly

4. Pedro's _**clownish**_ act was really funny.
   (clown)   -ly -ish

5. The sun was shining, and the sky was _**cloudless**_.
   (cloud)   -less -ful

6. I can help you put some oil on this _**squeaky**_ door.
   (squeak)   -y -ly

7. The children watching the puppet show looked _**cheerful**_.
   (cheer)   -ish -ful

8. Billy is _**friendly**_ to all of his team members.
   (friend)   -ly -able

9. I will be _**truthful**_ and tell you how I feel.
   (truth)   -ful -less

10. Marta's new sweater is _**washable**_.
    (wash)   -less -able

Forming words with suffixes in context -ful, -less, -y, -ly, -able, -ish   135

REVIEW   Prefixes and Suffixes

Name _____

Read the clues. Add one of the prefixes or suffixes from the list to each underlined base word to form a word that matches the clue.

1. full of <u>truth</u>   _truthful_

2. having <u>frost</u>   frosty

3. the opposite of <u>agree</u>   disagree

4. to <u>write</u> again   rewrite

5. the opposite of <u>trust</u>   distrust

6. to <u>pay</u> before   prepay

7. without <u>pain</u>   painless

8. full of <u>care</u>   careful

pre-
dis-
re-
-ful
-less
-y

1. to <u>do</u> too much   overdo

2. not <u>true</u>   untrue

3. like a <u>child</u>   childish

4. <u>read</u> wrongly   misread

5. every <u>week</u>   weekly

6. able to <u>change</u>   changeable

7. to <u>sleep</u> too much   oversleep

8. not <u>hurt</u>   unhurt

un-
over-
mis-
-ly
-able
-ish

136   Review of forming words with prefixes and suffixes

Prefixes and Suffixes

Name _____

Read the list of words below. Circle the prefix or suffix in each word.

thought(ful) thank(less) read(able) (mis)treat
(green)(ish) (dis)connect fair(ly) (un)safe
(over)flow (re)place (pre)heat rust(y)

Read the list of words below. Then read the sentences that follow. Write the word from the list that makes sense in each sentence.

unpack helpless disappear rewrap restful misplace
rocky overload pregame neatly grayish breakable

1. The book about magic tricks shows you how to make a ball *disappear*.
2. There will be a _pregame_ show on the football field.
3. When Bill gets home, he will _unpack_ his suitcases.
4. Please _rewrap_ the leftover food and put it in the freezer.
5. We felt _helpless_ when we couldn't fix the car.
6. Climbing up the _rocky_ hillside took us most of the day.
7. Did you _misplace_ the books you brought home?
8. I will be careful when I wash the _breakable_ vase.
9. My new cat has a _grayish_ coat and white paws.
10. Because I felt ill, I was told to have a _restful_ day at home.
11. The books and papers are stacked _neatly_ on the shelves.
12. The truck will not run well if you _overload_ it.

Assessment of identifying prefixes and suffixes; Words containing prefixes and suffixes in context   137

Syllables

Name _____

Words to use: afternoon, always, begin, country, bottom, chipmunk, hungry, everyone, bark, library, move, summer, elephant, friendly, kitchen, telephone

Many words are made of small parts called syllables. Because each syllable has one vowel sound, a word has as many syllables as it has vowel sounds. The word **stone** has one vowel sound, so it has one syllable. The word **raincoat** has two vowel sounds, so it has two syllables.

Name the pictures. Write the number of syllables you hear in each picture name.

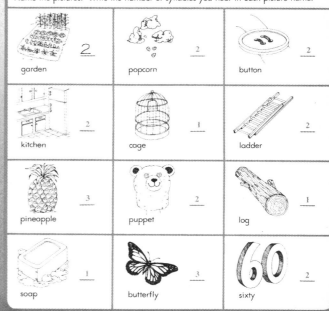

garden 2 | popcorn 2 | button 2
kitchen 2 | cage 1 | ladder 2
pineapple 3 | puppet 2 | log 1
soap 1 | butterfly 3 | sixty 2

138   Identifying the number of syllables in a word

Syllables

Name _____

Words to use: suntan, footprint, mailbox, bookcase, firewood, grandson, workbook, highway, bedspread, raincoat, necktie, seashell, pancakes, sunshine, airport, bluebird, airplane

A compound word should be divided into syllables between the words that make it compound.   rain/bow

Read the words below. Circle each compound word. Then write each compound word and draw a line between its syllables.

1. (sunset) *sun/set*
2. summer
3. (someone) some/one
4. (lighthouse) light/house
5. trouble
6. (notebook) note/book
7. (highway) high/way
8. jumping
9. broom
10. (railroad) rail/road
11. (starfish) star/fish
12. spray
13. (doghouse) dog/house
14. (baseball) base/ball
15. (homemade) home/made
16. (puppy)
17. (without) with/out
18. (bedroom) bed/room
19. (teapot) tea/pot
20. (birthday) birth/day
21. (toothbrush) tooth/brush
22. (raindrop) rain/drop
23. (lifeboat) life/boat
24. (sidewalk) side/walk
25. (snowflake) snow/flake
26. throat
27. (downtown) down/town
28. father

Identifying and dividing compound words into syllables   139

Syllables

Name _____

Words to use: unfair, rewrap, preheat, hopeless, quickly, undo, replace, overlook, overload, mistreat, misplace, reachable, yellowish, girlish, washable, oversteep, untrue, unzip, repaid

A word that has a prefix or suffix can be divided into syllables between the prefix or suffix and the base word.   un/tie   dark/ness

Read the list of words and the sentences. Divide each list word into syllables by drawing a line between the syllables. Then write the word from the list that makes sense in each sentence.

un/tie
pre/test
sleep/less
thought/ful
re/fill
dis/like
neat/ly
soft/ly
re/write
rain/y

1. Today I will *rewrite* my story with a pen.
2. We will _refill_ the car's gas tank before we start on our trip.
3. Please help me _untie_ this string so I can open the box.
4. I will sing the song _softly_ to the baby.
5. Before he started the lesson, the teacher gave us a _pretest_ to see what we knew.
6. Calling me on my birthday was a _thoughtful_ thing for you to do.
7. Because the dog barked for many hours, I had a _sleepless_ night.
8. I _dislike_ walking to school on rainy days.
9. It is hard to ride a bike on a _rainy_ day.
10. All of the books were _neatly_ placed on the shelves.

140   Dividing words containing affixes into syllables; Using two-syllable words in context

202

Syllables

Name

When a word has two consonants between two vowels, the word is usually divided between the two consonants.

mon/key	cir/cus
VC/CV	VC/CV

Read the list of words. Write each word and draw a line between its syllables.

1.	magnet	*mag/net*	6.	corner	cor/ner
2.	blanket	blan/ket	7.	mistake	mis/take
3.	harvest	har/vest	8.	happen	hap/pen
4.	lumber	lum/ber	9.	basket	bas/ket
5.	butter	but/ter	10.	dentist	den/tist

Read each sentence and the words below each blank. Complete each sentence by writing the word that has the VC/CV pattern. Draw a line between its syllables.

1. Last *win/ter* we went to see Grandmother and Grandfather.
   (weekend, winter)

2. We can buy food for the picnic at the _____ mar/ket _____.
   (market, store)

3. Did you leave a _____ pen/cil _____ on my desk this morning?
   (paper, pencil)

4. The _____ prin/cess _____ sometimes wears a fancy crown.
   (lady, princess)

5. Place a _____ nap/kin _____ next to each plate on the table.
   (napkin, fork)

6. The baby held a _____ sil/ver _____ spoon in her hand.
   (tiny, silver)

Syllables

Name

Words that have one consonant between two vowels can be divided into syllables in two ways. When you see a word that has one consonant between two vowels, say the word. If the first vowel sound is long, divide the word after the first vowel. If the first vowel sound is short, divide the word after the consonant that follows the vowel.

1	ē/ven	pā/per
	V/CV	V/CV
2	vĭs/it	mĕt/al
	VC/V	VC/V

Read the list of words. Write each word. Mark the first vowel of the word with ˘ if it stands for the short sound or ¯ if it stands for the long sound. Then draw a line between its syllables.

1.	label	*lā/bel*	11.	pupil	pu/pil
2.	moment	mo/ment	12.	petal	pĕt/al
3.	cabin	cab/in	13.	fever	fē/ver
4.	lemon	lem/on	14.	planet	plan/et
5.	travel	trav/el	15.	finish	fin/ish
6.	music	mu/sic	16.	famous	fā/mous
7.	open	o/pen	17.	siren	si/ren
8.	salad	sal/ad	18.	pedal	pĕd/al
9.	robin	rob/in	19.	tiger	ti/ger
10.	silent	si/lent	20.	wagon	wag/on

Syllables

Name

Read the list of words. Write each word and draw a line between its syllables. Mark the first vowel of the word with ˘ if it stands for the short sound or ¯ if it stands for the long sound.

1.	camel	*căm/el*	6.	closet	clŏs/et
2.	acorn	ā/corn	7.	famous	fā/mous
3.	palace	păl/ace	8.	medal	mĕd/al
4.	damage	dăm/age	9.	bacon	bā/con
5.	paper	pā/per	10.	minus	mi/nus

Read the list of words and the sentences. Divide each list word into syllables by drawing a line between the syllables. Then write the word from the list that makes sense in each sentence.

hu/man
sec/ond
shad/ow
fla/vor
hab/it
po/ny
pi/lot
shiv/er
met/al
ho/tel

1. I learned how to ride a *pony* when I was young.

2. Greg won _____ second _____ prize in the art contest.

3. Our room in the _____ hotel _____ is big enough for the whole family.

4. The _____ pilot _____ can fly the airplane at night.

5. Choose the _____ flavor _____ of ice cream you like best.

6. The shed is made of wood and _____ metal _____.

7. Packing an apple in my lunch is a _____ habit _____ for me.

8. Each February we wait to see if the groundhog will see its _____ shadow _____.

Syllables

Name

Read the words below. Write each word and draw a line between its syllables.

1.	chapter	*chap/ter*	17.	doorbell	door/bell
2.	undress	un/dress	18.	notice	no/tice
3.	cozy	co/zy	19.	painless	pain/less
4.	squeaky	squeak/y	20.	distrust	dis/trust
5.	magic	mag/ic	21.	lemon	lem/on
6.	hopeless	hope/less	22.	sunny	sun/ny
7.	firewood	fire/wood	23.	highway	high/way
8.	model	mod/el	24.	later	la/ter
9.	picnic	pic/nic	25.	harbor	har/bor
10.	truthful	truth/ful	26.	wishbone	wish/bone
11.	button	but/ton	27.	reuse	re/use
12.	oatmeal	oat/meal	28.	salad	sal/ad
13.	closet	clos/et	29.	acorn	a/corn
14.	pretest	pre/test	30.	slowly	slow/ly
15.	never	nev/er	31.	unsafe	un/safe
16.	minus	mi/nus	32.	rewrite	re/write

Syllables

Name _____

Read the words below. Write each word and draw a line between its syllables.

1. refill   _re/fill_   6. displease   _dis/please_
2. friendly _friend/ly_   7. pencil   _pen/cil_
3. yellow   _yel/low_   8. notebook   _note/book_
4. human   _hu/man_   9. petal   _pet/al_
5. untie   _un/tie_   10. cheerful   _cheer/ful_

Read the list of words and the sentences. Divide each list word into syllables by drawing a line between the syllables. Then write the word from the list that makes sense in each sentence.

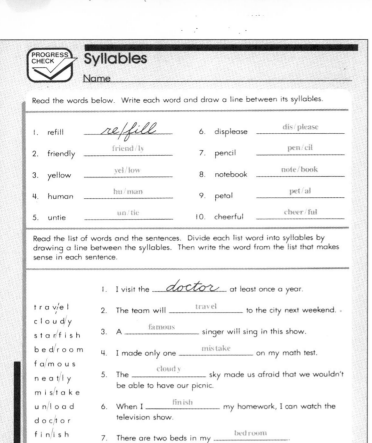

t r a v/e l
c l o u d/y
s t a r/f i s h
b e d/r o o m
f a/m o u s
n e a t/l y
m i s/t a k e
u n/l o a d
d o c/t o r
f i n/i s h

1. I visit the _doctor_ at least once a year.
2. The team will _travel_ to the city next weekend.
3. A _famous_ singer will sing in this show.
4. I made only one _mistake_ on my math test.
5. The _cloudy_ sky made us afraid that we wouldn't be able to have our picnic.
6. When I _finish_ my homework, I can watch the television show.
7. There are two beds in my _bedroom_.
8. Please help us _unload_ the boxes from the truck.

Reading and Writing Wrap-Up

Name _____

Safety Rules

Read the following important rules for street safety. Follow these rules yourself and help others follow them, too.

1. Cross streets only at the corners.
2. Always look both ways before you cross the street.
3. Do not cross the street when the light is red. Wait until the light turns to green.
4. Do not walk between parked cars.
5. Always walk on the left side of the road, facing the cars.
6. Stop, look, and listen before you cross the railroad tracks. Be sure no train is coming.
7. Do not ride your bicycle on the sidewalk.
8. Help little children cross the street safely.
9. Do not get into a car with a stranger.
10. Find a police officer when you see trouble.

A. Finish each rule with the right word or words.

1. Cross only at ___corners___.
2. ___Stop___, ___look___, and ___listen___ before you cross the railroad tracks.
3. Never get into a car with a ___stranger___.
4. Don't ride your bicycle on the ___sidewalk___.
5. Walk on the ___left___ side of the road, ___facing___ the cars.
6. When you see trouble, you should find a ___police officer___.
7. Before you cross the street, you should look ___both___ ways.

Name _____

Health

B. Finish each idea in your own words.

Answers may vary. Suggested answers are given.

1. A police officer is someone who _can help you_
2. A stranger is someone _you don't know_
3. A red light means _stop_
4. A green light means _go_

C. Think about these questions. Write answers for two of them.
   Why should you walk on the left side of the road, facing the cars?
   Why shouldn't you walk between parked cars?
   Why should you stop, look, and listen before you cross the railroad tracks?
   Why shouldn't you ride your bicycle on the sidewalk?

Answers will vary but might include the following ideas.

1. _You should walk on the left side of the road, facing the cars, so you can see what's coming on your side of the road._

   You shouldn't walk between parked cars because drivers might not be able to see you.

2. _You should stop, look, and listen before you cross the railroad tracks to be sure no train is coming._

   You shouldn't ride your bicycle on the sidewalk because you might injure other people.

Antonyms

Name _____

An antonym is a word that has the opposite meaning of another word.

Words to use: light -heavy, everything -nothing, loose -tight, cool -warm, true -untrue, fat -thin, bright -dull, tame -wild, large -tiny, full -empty, noisy -quiet

early - late

Read the words in each box below. Draw a line to match each word with its antonym (opposite).

large — old	few — many	slow — hot
young — weak	off — after	cold — fast
strong — small	before — on	over — under
save — bumpy	always — fair	day — night
smooth — spend	unfair — dry	yes — no
early — late	wet — never	frown — smile

Read the list of words below. Then read the sentences that follow. Write the word from the list that is an antonym (opposite) for the underlined word in each sentence.

light   unkind   shut   shout
false   to   down   awake

1. This letter is from Uncle Todd.   _to_
2. I was asleep when Grandfather called.   _awake_
3. Is this living room always so dark?   _light_
4. Please help me open this heavy door.   _shut_
5. I will whisper the clue to you.   _shout_
6. Is the answer to this question true?   _false_
7. Please walk up the steps with me.   _down_
8. Writing that letter was kind.   _unkind_

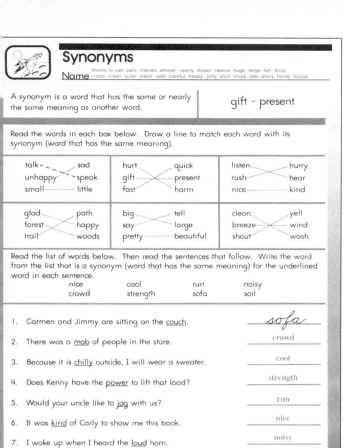

Synonyms

Name _____

Words to use: pals–friends, almost–nearly, dozen–twelve, huge–large, fall–drop, creep–crawl, quiet–silent, safe–careful, happy–jolly, shut–close, tale–story, home–house

A synonym is a word that has the same or nearly the same meaning as another word.

gift – present

Read the words in each box below. Draw a line to match each word with its synonym (word that has the same meaning).

talk — sad	hurt — quick	listen — hurry
unhappy — speak	gift — present	rush — hear
small — little	fast — harm	nice — kind

glad — path	big — tell	clean — yell
forest — happy	say — large	breeze — wind
trail — woods	pretty — beautiful	shout — wash

Read the list of words below. Then read the sentences that follow. Write the word from the list that is a synonym (word that has the same meaning) for the underlined word in each sentence.

nice   cool   run   noisy
crowd   strength   sofa   soil

1. Carmen and Jimmy are sitting on the <u>couch</u>.   *sofa*
2. There was a <u>mob</u> of people in the store.   crowd
3. Because it is <u>chilly</u> outside, I will wear a sweater.   cool
4. Does Kenny have the <u>power</u> to lift that load?   strength
5. Would your uncle like to <u>jog</u> with us?   run
6. It was <u>kind</u> of Carly to show me this book.   nice
7. I woke up when I heard the <u>loud</u> horn.   noisy
8. Do you have enough <u>dirt</u> for that plant?   soil

Identifying synonyms   149

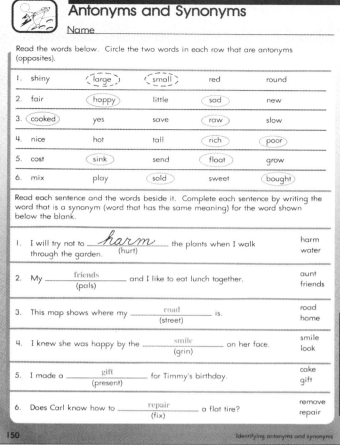

Antonyms and Synonyms

Name _____

Read the words below. Circle the two words in each row that are antonyms (opposites).

1. shiny   (large) (small) red round
2. fair   (happy) little (sad) new
3. (cooked) yes save (raw) slow
4. nice   hot tall (rich) (poor)
5. cost   (sink) send (float) grow
6. mix   play (sold) sweet (bought)

Read each sentence and the words beside it. Complete each sentence by writing the word that is a synonym (word that has the same meaning) for the word shown below the blank.

1. I will try not to *harm* the plants when I walk through the garden. (hurt)   harm / water
2. My __friends__ and I like to eat lunch together. (pals)   aunt / friends
3. This map shows where my __road__ is. (street)   road / home
4. I knew she was happy by the __smile__ on her face. (grin)   smile / look
5. I made a __gift__ for Timmy's birthday. (present)   cake / gift
6. Does Carl know how to __repair__ a flat tire? (fix)   remove / repair

150   Identifying antonyms and synonyms

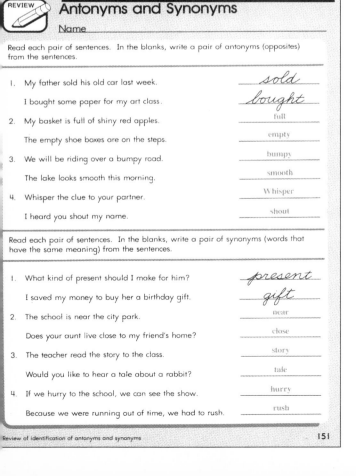

REVIEW

Antonyms and Synonyms

Name _____

Read each pair of sentences. In the blanks, write a pair of antonyms (opposites) from the sentences.

1. My father sold his old car last week.   *sold*
   I bought some paper for my art class.   *bought*
2. My basket is full of shiny red apples.   full
   The empty shoe boxes are on the steps.   empty
3. We will be riding over a bumpy road.   bumpy
   The lake looks smooth this morning.   smooth
4. Whisper the clue to your partner.   Whisper
   I heard you shout my name.   shout

Read each pair of sentences. In the blanks, write a pair of synonyms (words that have the same meaning) from the sentences.

1. What kind of present should I make for him?   *present*
   I saved my money to buy her a birthday gift.   *gift*
2. The school is near the city park.   near
   Does your aunt live close to my friend's home?   close
3. The teacher read the story to the class.   story
   Would you like to hear a tale about a rabbit?   tale
4. If we hurry to the school, we can see the show.   hurry
   Because we were running out of time, we had to rush.   rush

Review of identification of antonyms and synonyms   151

PROGRESS CHECK

Antonyms and Synonyms

Name _____

Read the list of words below. Then read the sentences that follow. Write the word from the list that is an antonym (opposite) for the underlined word in each sentence.

never   float   late
strong   save   bought

1. I would like to <u>spend</u> some money this year.   *save*
2. Am I here too <u>early</u> to see the show?   late
3. Jake <u>always</u> brings his lunch from home.   never
4. The toy boat will <u>sink</u> when you put it in the water.   float
5. Running races has made my legs feel <u>weak</u>.   strong
6. I <u>sold</u> baskets of flowers at the market.   bought

Read the list of words below. Then read the sentences that follow. Write the word from the list that is a synonym (word that has the same meaning) for the underlined word in each sentence.

unhappy   cool   glad
present   path   pretty

1. I felt <u>sad</u> when my friend moved.   *unhappy*
2. The colored lights of the city look <u>beautiful</u>.   pretty
3. He made the painting as a <u>gift</u> for his uncle.   present
4. The wind makes me feel <u>chilly</u>.   cool
5. I am <u>happy</u> that you could be with us today.   glad
6. This <u>trail</u> leads to some picnic tables.   path

152   Assessment of identifying antonyms and synonyms in context

Homophones

Name _____

Words to use: piece-peace, hall-haul, would-wood, soar-sore, son-sun, blue-blew, beat-beet, ring-wring, in-inn, through-threw, or-oar

Homophones are words that sound the same but have different spellings and different meanings.

would - wood

Read the words. Draw a line to match each word with its homophone (word that sounds the same).

your	tow	night	knight	week	hear
toe	you're	knew	tale	here	sent
wait	weight	tail	new	cent	pale
too	sale	deer	dear	pail	weak
sail	two	maid	made	sea	see

Read each pair of sentences. In the blanks, write a pair of homophones (words that sound the same) from the sentences.

1. The book you want is on the right side of the shelf.

   Please write a letter to me soon.

   right
   write

2. My nose always gets sunburned when I'm at the beach.

   Edward knows the way to the new classroom.

   nose
   knows

3. Where can I buy some fishing line for my new rod?

   We went by the street where you used to live.

   buy
   by

4. There is a big knot in that jump rope.

   Penny will not be running in the next race.

   knot
   not

5. Before I bake bread, I must buy some flour.

   The flower will look nice in this tall yellow vase.

   flour
   flower

Homographs

Name _____

Homographs are words that have the same spelling but different meanings. Sometimes they are pronounced differently.

Those old pipes are made of **lead.**   Jack will **lead** the band.

Read each pair of sentences and circle the homographs (words that have the same spelling). Then draw a line from each sentence to the picture it tells about.

 Connie will show us how to (wind) the clock.
The (wind) made the trees bend near the water.

 I could feel the tree's rough (bark).
The dog will (bark) when it sees you.

 In the play, he must slowly (bow) to the queen.
Debbie tied a large (bow) onto the birthday gift.

 Please (tear) the paper into two pieces.
A tiny (tear) fell from the baby's eye.

 Jack will (close) the door of the car.
Annie stood (close) to the basketball hoop.

Homophones and Homographs

Name _____

Read the words below. Circle the two words in each row that are homophones (words that sound the same).

1.	been	(bear)	bake	(bare)	bale
2.	(beat)	beak	bead	(beet)	bean
3.	sink	(cent)	seem	center	(scent)
4.	(I)	I've	(eye)	egg	elf
5.	send	(sea)	(see)	sell	seat
6.	heat	head	he	(heal)	(heel)

Read the homographs (words that have the same spelling) and their meanings below. Then read the sentences that follow. In each sentence, decide the meaning of the underlined homograph. Write the letter of the correct meaning in the blank.

lead
A. a heavy metal
B. to show the way

tear
A. to rip
B. a drop of water from the eye

close
A. to shut
B. near

1. The pipes in the old building are made of lead. _A_

2. Did I see a tear fall from your eye? _B_

3. Russell stood close to his sister. _B_

4. Who will lead us to the lake? _B_

5. Please close the book when you are done reading the chapter. _A_

6. Use the edge of the box to tear the wrapping paper. _A_

Homophones and Homographs

Name _____

Read each pair of sentences. In the blanks, write a pair of homophones (words that sound the same) from the sentences.

1. I knew you would like to go walking through the city.

   The tall building you see on this street is new.

   knew
   new

2. Please meet me at the school lunchroom.

   What kind of meat should I use in the soup?

   meet
   meat

3. Carry the water in a little pail.

   When I was sick, my face looked pale.

   pail
   pale

4. You may use this oar in the rowboat.

   Come to my house before or after lunch.

   oar
   or

5. I will be sailing for eight days.

   The puppy ate all of its food today.

   eight
   ate

Read the list of homographs (words that have the same spelling) below. Then read each pair of meanings that follows. Write the homograph from the list that matches both meanings.

wind   bark   close   tear   bow   lead

1. A. to bend the head or body   B. a knot made of ribbon   *bow*

2. A. to shut   B. near   close

3. A. moving air   B. to turn or tighten   wind

4. A. water from the eye   B. to rip   tear

Homophones and Homographs

Name _____

Read each pair of sentences. In the blanks, write a pair of homophones (words that sound the same) from the sentences.

1. The cut will heal quickly if it is kept clean.

   My left shoe needs a new heel.

   heal
   heel

2. She knew the answer to the question.

   I found the new book on the top of the bookshelf.

   knew
   new

3. I rode to the woods on a brown pony.

   Which road leads to the shopping center?

   rode
   road

4. The bear cubs in the zoo are so playful.

   I walked in the sand in my bare feet.

   bear
   bare

Read the homographs (words that have the same spelling) and their meanings below. Then read the sentences that follow. In each sentence, decide the meaning of the underlined homograph. Write the letter of the correct meaning in the blank.

wind	bow	tear
A. moving air	A. to bend the head or body	A. to rip
B. to turn or twist	B. a knot made of ribbon	B. a drop of water from the eye

1. You need to <u>wind</u> the key on that toy to make it work. __B__

2. Please put a yellow <u>bow</u> on that gift. __B__

3. How did you <u>tear</u> your shirt? __A__

4. The <u>wind</u> blew the leaves across the lawn. __A__

Alphabetical Order

Name _____

You can put words in alphabetical order by looking at the first letter of each word. If the first letters of the words are the same, look at the second letters. If the second letters of the words are the same, look at the third letters.

dr**a**nk
dr**i**ve
dr**u**m

Read the lists of words. Number each list of words in alphabetical order.

List 1		List 2		List 3		List 4	
nail	1	price	5	clean	4	bring	4
nut	6	paint	1	city	3	blink	2
nine	4	pink	2	crown	6	broke	5
next	2	put	6	call	1	black	1
night	3	plum	3	coin	5	bread	3
noise	5	pond	4	cent	2	brush	6

Read the groups of words. Write each group of words in alphabetical order.

cream　crumb　cry
cross　crack

hide　home　heat
hall　hunt

shelf　shine　shoe
shut　sharp

1. *crack*	1. hall	1. sharp
2. cream	2. heat	2. shelf
3. cross	3. hide	3. shine
4. crumb	4. home	4. shoe
5. cry	5. hunt	5. shut

Guide Words

Name _____

The two words at the top of a dictionary page are called guide words. The first guide word is the same as the first word listed on the page. The second guide word is the same as the last word listed on the page. To find a word in the dictionary, decide if it comes in alphabetical order between the guide words on a page. If it does, you will find the word on that page.

Read each pair of guide words and the words that are listed below them. Circle the four words in each list that could be found on a page that has those guide words.

draw / foil	melt / pony	boat / cone
dime	(past)	crown
(drink)	(open)	(bride)
(face)	match	(cloud)
from	prize	(call)
(dust)	(must)	(chain)
(fire)	(nine)	cut

get / heavy	rose / stand	two / wrote
(grow)	rich	tractor
(happy)	(slide)	turtle
house	(rush)	(under)
icy	(scarf)	(voice)
(give)	(some)	(world)
(goat)	return	(wind)

Guide Words

Name _____

Read the six pairs of guide words and their dictionary page numbers. Then read the lists of words that follow. Write the page number on which each list word would be found in the dictionary.

apple / bend—p. 6　　**both / bunch**—p. 8　　**flight / give**—p. 26
glove / happy—p. 28　　**roar / send**—p. 46　　**sink / use**—p. 48

1. as	*p. 6*	13. branch	p. 8
2. smell	p. 48	14. geese	p. 26
3. gaze	p. 26	15. rust	p. 46
4. bright	p. 8	16. brown	p. 8
5. breeze	p. 8	17. art	p. 6
6. goat	p. 28	18. grape	p. 28
7. sand	p. 46	19. rug	p. 46
8. grown	p. 28	20. fresh	p. 26
9. band	p. 6	21. bark	p. 6
10. speak	p. 48	22. sold	p. 48
11. base	p. 6	23. rule	p. 46
12. those	p. 48	24. guess	p. 28

Panel 1 (page 161)

Guide Words

Name _____

Read the lists of words below. Then read the guide words that follow. Write each list word below the correct pair of guide words. Then number each list of words to show how they would be listed in alphabetical order.

bench	cane	lunch	change	must
leave	ashes	my	born	city
buy	make	oak	law	barn
noise	nice	answer	chew	lime

Words may be listed in any order.

1. above / broke

bench	4
ashes	2
answer	1
born	5
barn	3

2. butter / corn

buy	1
cane	2
change	3
chew	4
city	5

3. lamb / mice

leave	2
make	5
lunch	4
law	1
lime	3

4. mountain / old

noise	4
nice	3
my	2
oak	5
must	1

Using guide words; Alphabetizing by first, second, and third letters   161

Panel 2 (page 162)

Guide Words

Name _____

Read each pair of guide words and the words that are listed below them. Circle the four words in each list that could be found on a page that has those guide words.

held / ink	**jeep / leave**	**mist / nine**	**seat / such**
hall	(large)	(monkey)	(shelf)
(hide)	jail	march	(south)
(ice)	(join)	(name)	(spare)
(horse)	(judge)	melt	science
(howl)	(June)	(myself)	swing
itself	lift	(neat)	(smoke)

Read the four pairs of guide words and their dictionary page numbers. Then read the lists of words that follow. Write the page number on which each list word would be found in the dictionary.

above / are—p. 1   **arm / blue**—p. 2
both / child—p. 5   **cord / dime**—p. 7

1. ate	*p. 2*	8. always	p. 1	15. dawn	p. 7
2. add	p. 1	9. bush	p. 5	16. bunk	p. 5
3. cost	p. 7	10. air	p. 1	17. aunt	p. 2
4. brick	p. 5	11. desk	p. 7	18. chest	p. 5
5. awake	p. 2	12. angry	p. 1	19. curl	p. 7
6. being	p. 2	13. apple	p. 1	20. cent	p. 5
7. animal	p. 1	14. base	p. 2	21. creek	p. 7

162   Review of using guide words

Panel 3 (page 163)

PROGRESS CHECK

Guide Words

Name _____

Read the lists of words below. Then read the guide words that follow. Write each list word below the correct pair of guide words. Then number each list of words to show how they would be listed in alphabetical order.

knee	heat	valley	idea	twelve
high	upon	listen	its	ice
uncle	jam	lace	jelly	job
lead	lump	hope	join	us

Words may be listed in any order.

1. harm / inch

high	2
heat	1
hope	3
idea	5
ice	4

2. is / kept

jam	2
its	1
jelly	3
join	5
job	4

3. kind / mercy

knee	1
lead	3
lump	5
listen	4
lace	2

4. turn / village

uncle	2
upon	3
valley	5
twelve	1
us	4

Assessment of using guide words; Alphabetizing by first, second, and third letters   163

Panel 4 (page 164)

Reading and Writing Wrap-Up

Name _____

Weather

Everyone talks about the weather, but no one does anything about it. Have you ever heard this saying? There's not much anyone *can* do about the weather. Would you like to have a picnic or go swimming? Do you want to go ice skating or ride your sled? The weather may decide what you can do.

Hot and Cold

In many places, it is hot in the summer. In the winter, it is cold. In the spring and fall, it may be warm on some days and cool on others. Knowing if it will be hot, warm, cool, or cold can help you decide how to dress and what kind of work or play you can do.

Wind

Air that moves sideways is called wind. A wind that blows from the north is cold, and a wind that blows from the south may be warm. The speed of the wind can change the weather.

Clouds

The clouds in the sky can also change the weather. There are different kinds of clouds. Many people can tell from the kind of clouds in the sky what the weather is going to be like. Some clouds mean rain; other clouds mean fair weather.

1. Check the word that tells the main idea.

_____ picnics   ✓ weather   _____ clouds

2. Check each group of words that tells something that can change the weather.

✓ the speed of the wind

_____ the kind of clothes you wear

✓ the kind of clouds in the sky

164   Application of reading and comprehension skills in a science context